RITE OF PASSAGE

RITE OF PASSAGE

How to Teach Your Son about
Sex and Manhood

E. James Wilder

Servant Publications
Ann Arbor, Michigan

Copyright © 1990 and 1994 by E. James Wilder
All rights reserved.

Vine Books is an imprint of Servant Publications especially
designed to serve evangelical Christians.

This book was first published as *Just between Father & Son* by
InterVarsity Press in 1990
P.O. Box 1400
Downers Grove, Illinois 60516

This revised and expanded version is published by
Servant Publications
P.O. Box 8617
Ann Arbor, Michigan 48107

All Scripture quotations are from *The New English Bible* © 1961
and 1970 by the Delegates of Oxford University Press and the
Syndics of Cambridge University Press. Reprinted with permission.

Cover design by Michael Andaloro
Cover photograph by Howard M. DeCruyenaere
Interior illustrations by Roberta Polfus

94 95 96 97 98   10 9 8 7 6 5 4 3 2 1

Printed in the United States of America
ISBN 0-89283-873-6

Library of Congress Cataloging-in-Publication Data

Wilder, E. James
    Rite of passage : how to teach your son about sex and man-
hood / E. James Wilder.
        p. cm.
    Rev. and expanded ed. of: Just between father & son. ©1990
    ISBN 0-89283-873-6
    1. Sex—Religious aspects—Christianity. 2. Men (Christian
theology) 3. Teenagers—Religious life. 4. Sex instruction for
children—Religious aspects—Christianity. I. Wilder, E. James,
1952—   Just between father & son. II. Title.
BT708.W47 1994
248.8'421—dc20   93-46844

CONTENTS

THANKS AND ACKNOWLEDGMENTS

MANY PEOPLE have shaped my life. This is their story as well. All the stories in this book are true. Some names and places have been changed to protect both the innocent and guilty. Where real names are used these people have agreed to share their lives with you as they have with me. Please honor their trust with respect and love.

Even my life is here by permission. My sexual life is my wife's garden, hers to enjoy. She has tended well what I gave her when it was still full of weeds. Those of you who read my story do so with her invitation.

Finally, you will enter my children's inner lives and thoughts. We have spent a long time talking with them about the ramifications of inviting people to see what they may not have seen in their own offspring. With the exuberance of youth, my sons have given what you now hold.

Blessed are those who come in peace. Welcome to our home.

The preparation of this book has brought me support from many people to whom I am deeply grateful. Kitty, my wife, has helped me to clarify the issues and with proofreading. My mother labored diligently editing and praying about the manuscript. My father provided support, along with his vehement disagreement with some of my views. The word processor on which this was written and some of the resource material are from my brother Tim, who objects to my "confessional" style.

Dick Birkey's timely and thoughtful corrections make him a valued friend.

The staff at Shepherd's House Family Counseling Center where I am director of training has greatly encouraged, supported, challenged, and cared for me over the years. Margie Keyser and Rick Koepcke have been particularly thorough in reviewing this work.

There is a special place here for the clients who visit my office each week. One dear lady who has been sexually abused by dozens of men since infancy struggled through these pages seeking a world she had never known. She has made a painful investment in this handbook for the training of young men so that others may escape her fate.

We owe a particular debt of gratitude to the late Walter Trobisch. His books and his warm, open treatment of sexuality have greatly changed our home. Kitty and I are among those who have received his counsel in person and our intimate life together has been much richer for it. In addition, it was Walter who first encouraged me, by a letter, to seek graduate training in counseling. To us he is "Papa Trobisch."

Introduction

WHAT IS A RITE OF PASSAGE?

At critical moments of our lives, we face changes so profound that they can be said to refashion who we are. Our birth, the death of a loved one, our first child, or our first sexual experience are such times. But few profound changes come at a worse time than puberty—the coming of age of an adolescent. This passage marks the change from childhood to adulthood and would seem at first to have very little going for it. It gives children a new self complete with adult bodies, minds, emotions, and powers right in the middle of awkwardness, squeaky voices, and "blemishes." It arrives for the prepared and the unprepared alike.

Traditional societies have had the wisdom to provide a bit of training and guidance during the momentous passage from childhood to adulthood. These training tools have been built into their cultures for just this need. The elders of these communities guide boys into a new sense of themselves as men, thus allowing boys a way to intelligently and knowingly become men. This time of training, preparation, and change, along with its requirements and rituals, has been called a "rite of passage."

In search of new land, knowledge, and independence,

Western peoples have come to deplore any indoctrination into the "old ways," preferring instead to question authority and seek new ways. Traditions, whether intelligent, needed, or simply misunderstood, have suffered disregard as a result. These days few men know when or if they ever successfully made the transition to manhood. Most men are at a loss helping boys make the transition as well. The men's movement has called for the community of men to rediscover this transforming task, but for most boys the rite of passage will depend on their parents' efforts. I was one such parent. My two sons are now men, and I am glad I took the time to see them through their rites of passage. It didn't go perfectly for either of them. I'm just one father who worked with the support of his wife. Yet that was enough.

TELLING YOUR SON ABOUT SEX

The one part of a rite of passage which still receives a fair amount of attention is telling boys the "facts of life." This book will really help fathers become comfortable, even happy, telling their sons about sex. This job is best done by a boy's father, but when that is neither possible nor desirable, mothers and male relatives, youth leaders, teachers, doctors, and others will have to fill the void. If for some reason the job should fall to a mother, she can use this book as a guide to what a father would do. If a mother seeks the help of male relatives, this book will help prepare them to share the secrets of life with her son. One thing is sure, the boy who is helped through this passage will never forget his guides, whether they are good, bad, or inattentive.

Manhood always arrives one way or another for boys. Puberty strikes whether there is a dad available and involved or not. Many times mothers are left to make the best of a situation that is imperfect due to the absence or inadequacy of their husbands. Single mothers often face their sons' adolescence with a particular sense of loss. They share with their sons the absence of the man who should be there to love and guide them. Growing up is hard enough, but with the loss of a dad or his lack of involvement, boys face additional strains. It is difficult for them to know whether to be angry, sad, lonely, or even relieved at Dad's absence.

It is also hard to know exactly how much difference a father's absence will make in a son's life. If the mother is well connected to her community, there will be many men, such as her father, brothers, cousins, uncles, and grandfathers, along with the elders of the community, to welcome her son among the society of men. Ideally, this community will include a lively and committed church with elders who are spiritual fathers to the young. The loss of a father is painful, but if the boy is motivated and his community accepting, he can still come out better than a boy with an indifferent father who is home every night.

Mothers often worry about their children. The more a mother wishes that her son will not turn out like his father, the more she has to worry about. While a much more complete description of how to raise a son can be found in my book, *Life Passages for Men*, there still is no perfect way to raise a boy. There is also no perfect way to take a boy through the rite of passage into manhood. Frustration follows those who can only do things "the right way." In this case, providing a rite of passage in a culture which has no accepted and culturally approved guidelines leaves us little with which to judge the right way. This disturbs thoughtful parents. Perhaps this will change someday. Until then, though, there can be no single right way for boys to become men.

On the other hand, there is nothing a young man would like better than to be appreciated by a dad he respects. We do know that this rite of passage is accomplished through affirmation. Boys can become men by being affirmed as men when the time is right.

Affirmations can be made by both women and men. One

friend of mine found his masculinity most affirmed by the admiration of his aunt. She told him how good his broad shoulders looked and complimented him in other ways. He survived on this bit of affirmation for twenty-five years until the men in his life could do their part. While a woman helped him through puberty, obviously, only men could welcome him as one of their own.

Much can be achieved by anyone, whether male or female, relative or friend, who can sincerely say to a young man, "You're a fine young man, and I really enjoy and admire this or that about you. You are wonderful that way." Almost any notice is better by far than none. If you appreciate your son, don't be embarrassed to say so; there are no perfect lives. It would be far better to have a rite of passage by an appreciative mother or aunt than none at all.

Still, attention from only one parent, be it father or mother, always has its price. In particular, when this notice comes only from males or females, it leaves any teenager with some vulnerability. It has long been established that girls seek endorsement from their fathers in order to establish their own femininity. Yet even those who receive their father's approval and face rejection by their mother are in serious trouble. They will struggle trying to become women. Likewise, men deprived of acceptance by their fathers face a colossal battle. Full victory for a teenager will only be achieved with the help of both men and women who believe in *them*.

Too often teens discover that this support comes only from their peers who are, in a sense, still children. Peer support is better than nothing, but those who give affirmation and support during a rite of passage receive the right to help define the boy's new identity as a man. Helping another child through a rite of passage is a task that children will never do adequately, because none of them can possibly know what a man really is.

I hope that my example of how to celebrate a rite of passage will inform or even inspire men and women to try something like it with their children. So let us not fear the rite of passage but become its supporters. Whether you are a child, teenager, woman, or man, your affirmation may well be the "first aid" that helps a young man or woman through a crisis until they reach the arms of the men and women who ultimately must say welcome.

Even women whose husbands are willing and able to help their sons have a key role in this time of growth. Many men will receive no support in affirming their son's manhood and sexuality except from their wives. By reading this book, women will know how to encourage their husbands' efforts. No men took me aside with directions on how to help my sons; the awareness of their needs came first from their mother. It is no accident that the story in this book started as my dear wife's idea.

This story is really intended for adults. It is not meant to be given to children as a substitute for their own rite of passage, although it might be very good to give this book to both boys and girls as a part of their training. Girls as well as boys could benefit from reading about what it means to become a man. This, then, is not a book to hand to your son as his only guide to puberty. And yet this is a book about becoming a man— regardless of what your age may be.

What you can hope to find in these pages is one father's attempt to lead his sons into Christian manhood without blinders or pretenses. You will not find the ideal life or the ideal way to tell your children about what it means to grow up to be a man. Those who wish to will find flaws in my character, theology, judgment, knowledge, and methods. It isn't hard to do, I see several myself. I share about my own struggles with growing into Christian manhood and male sexuality to encourage others in their growth.

To women who read this, perhaps to encourage your husbands to try some of these ideas, I say, "Welcome!"

I am concerned, however, about people who are not in touch with their own sexuality and its power. They are a hazard to their families and communities. Those who deny their vulnerability or personal problems in this area are the ones who will cause the most damage. They will not have the patience and understanding needed to read this book with care.

I am concerned as well for people who have been victims of the misdirected sexuality of others. Most victims, whether they are male or female, have been the victims of men. You may find that a frank discussion of male sexuality causes you to feel fear, pain, or anger. These are normal, even healthy, reactions to trauma. This book is aimed more at prevention than healing past hurts. I believe that a healthy sexuality within God's specifications is the best preventative medicine there can be. Rest assured, though, that your plight is not forgotten.

For the men who read this book, I have a dream to share. I dream of honest men of integrity. It is time for us as men to reject the notion that we can't accept the truth, face emotional pain, and confront our problems because of a fragile male ego. We have used this fragile male ego myth to cover up our failures and avoid looking at ourselves. Thus, the women and children in our lives, who presumably have stronger egos than we have, must pick up the slack and take responsibility for our actions and feelings. Come on, guys! Let us at least try to struggle honestly with our problems. We need to accept responsibility for our actions, emotions, and shortcomings if we expect to learn and grow, especially if we want to pass on a legacy to our sons. No more hiding behind excuses. No more blaming others. No more hiding behind phrases like, "This is just the way I am." Let us have an honest look at who we are, for that is the best indication of who our sons will become.

I trust many of you will be able to relate, perhaps uncomfortably, to my struggles. Our sexuality is good if we can figure out how it is meant to work!

"So God created man in his own image; in the image of God he created them; male and female he created them. And so it was; and God saw all he had made and it was very good" (Gn 1:27, 31).

A REFLECTION BY JAMIE

Note to the reader: This reflection is written by my eldest son, Jamie, whose weekend trip with me six years ago formed the basis for this book. Jamie shares his thoughts here six years later as an eighteen-year-old who is in college. I include it here to indicate the kind of long-term benefit that can come from such a rite of passage and to give you a young man's perspective on the journey into manhood.

THE TRIP WITH MY FATHER was not a single event that suddenly transformed our relationship. It was, instead, a step that launched us into the next stage of who we were as father and son. Now it meant we were relating man to man. The trip itself was just an excerpt from our lives together. It came as the culmination of my childhood and the beginning of my adulthood. I now had enough knowledge and accountability to be dealt with as a man and to discuss issues like real men do.

The basis for the trip was not some awe-inspiring "this will answer your questions about life, Son" speech, but rather a dialogue about life. It gave my dad and me an opportunity to bring issues out into the open. We saw what I knew, what he knew, and what the two of us could learn. I opened up to my dad and showed him what I was thinking. In return, I learned in an in-depth way what my dad was really like. We talked about things that were important to us.

We talked about what my role should be. My dad began to show me what I really could expect out of life and what I could give to the world as opposed to take from it. He also showed me some of how I could expect the world to react to my behavior. God-fearing men have their place, but sometimes the world just doesn't like that.

I have learned about relationships from my father. He has given me insight into the real joy of loving and cherishing others. My dad has done the most for me by just living his life and showing me God through it. He shows me love, and I see it in his eyes. I wonder how he can be so wise.

Some of my friends fell into the standard traps and made mistakes that I avoided. When I saw compatriots attacking each other in junior high, I knew why. They were only trying to demonstrate their power. I already knew about the power I had, and I didn't need to try and find it by taking it out on my friends. My dad was good at showing me that I was powerful.

The same thing happened in high school. Everyone wanted to see if they could make the adults bow to them. I watched argument after argument erupt from this senseless confrontation with adult authority. I had an advantage over my peers when encountering these things that my dad had talked about. I knew what was happening when they didn't. I had the chance to think through my responses beforehand. I had a jump on the rest of them. They had surprises that threw them off, but I was able to enjoy these new wonderful experiences in life because I could gauge what was coming and handle it accordingly.

I was surprised at the letter I received from my good friend, Mark, who was in his senior year of high school. He told me that he had served time in juvenile hall for grand theft auto and fleeing from the police. He had decided to prove to his parents that they could not control him or dictate his life. His parents kicked him out, and Mark managed to stay at a friend's house until the court sentenced him.

Mark's parents didn't teach him about power, so he had to

find it on his own. That became very destructive. Mark says that I am the only friend that his parents will let him see. I think Mark is doing OK again; he is learning something about the use of power. It can be very overwhelming unless God is in control.

My dad had already been showing me that a real man uses his power to help others. God gave power to help and not to destroy. I knew that true power came from building each other up and helping others to heal. My family and my society were bigger structures that I wanted to contribute to, not "rape" for my own benefit.

The relationship between father and son is a vital link towards the continuation of life. Knowing one's father is knowing where you came from. You can learn from mistakes in the past which, although they are not your own, will affect you just the same. I learned when to ask questions. This didn't mean I was perfect, but the mistakes I made weren't as big and bad. I learned from my father's life.

I love my father. I treasure the times I spend with him. When I'm away, I miss the talks that we have. I don't know what I would do without his input and impact on my life. He shows me things in myself that I did not know were there and helps bring out my potential for greater things.

One night when I didn't know what to do with my feelings, he sat and talked with me. We stayed up late and discussed what was happening. He listened to my struggle and showed me my heart. He knew my plight; and without intruding into who I was, he helped me see God's hand in my life. I wish all fathers would do that.

As I start to move out on my own and thoughts of marriage and my own family cross my mind, I watch my father even more closely. I see how he reacts to my independence and the warnings that I get from him. He is doing a terrific job of letting go. He is still there for me, but he knows to wait until I ask for advice before giving it. He allows me my mistakes and trusts his raising of me.

I love the family that I come from and want to work hard at

creating my own based on the same principles. I watch how my father is and I want to be the same. My family is a part of me, and I want to keep it with me always. I want my kids to feel the same way that I do. I will always cherish what my dad has given me—a role model of what it means to be a man.

WHAT SHOULD ADULTS KNOW ABOUT ADOLESCENTS?

Adolescent men are intelligent. As unlikely as it seems at times, these twelve- to fifteen-year-old men are capable of thinking at an incredibly complex level. They can understand problems that face the world and start to come up with some solutions. Their answers might not be well thought through, but they are actual, real responses. They are growing as men.

As these men mature, they can start to deal with real emotions. They can feel just like you and me—the only difference being that they haven't been dealing with the emotions for as long as you and I have. Granted I am still learning, but so are you. These emotions are new to these men: they are finding out what the emotions mean, if others actually have them, and what to do about coping with them. I was always angered by the more adult world for not taking my emotions seriously, for deciding for me what I felt, and claiming I was "just going through something." Hormonal changes may increase or decrease emotions, but the emotions are still real.

Falling in love was a process that followed naturally from my development. Learning what really loving someone is about is a life-long process so, of course, I made mistakes about my feelings. But don't tell me I didn't *love*, just tell me I was *learning* what love meant. I was dealing with the world on an adult level. I was not preparing to deal with the world at an adult level. It was already too late for that. I was just making those beginning mistakes. A thirteen-year-old male is a man with a man's emotions and intellect. He should not be treated as a boy trying to become a man, but as a man discovering the things he needs to do and making his mistakes doing them.

Knowing that my mistakes were the efforts of a man has helped me learn and establish who I am. I know to look at what I have done; it has led to who I am and helped me decide what I want to do next. The relationship with my girlfriend that I blew at fifteen taught me things I will use in my coming marriage. Not a lot of guys my age are aware of the importance of this kind of reflection on their teenage years; to them it is a time of instantaneous pleasure, not of adult actions. They think that nothing they do matters until they turn eighteen, so they are still making the same mistakes they did at sixteen. While friends my age are still learning the basics of communicating, making decisions, seeing what they enjoy doing, what builds them up and satisfies in relationships and the other areas of life, I realize that I have a history and background of action as a man. These experiences help me relate with other men.

Adolescents are looking at the older men around them. They notice which ones are successful, and then try to emulate their successful characteristics. I learned about being a man from being treated as a man and experiencing what that means. When my dad treated me as a man and as I watched him act like a man with others, it gave me something to model and a direction in which to grow.

Men grow with men. A maturing male needs to be involved in a good Christian community. He needs to interact with people and learn from that experience. He will be a part of society for his entire life because that is what he is made for. This is where he will give and receive what is most important. This is where God will use him.

People respect my dad, and that means a lot to me. He once told me, "Boys want to be liked, but men want to be respected." Later he told me that he was proud of me because he saw I was trying to be respected to the point of risking not being liked.

Every man is unique and has more to offer than he knows. He is also powerful and needs to learn from the community how to use his power. God made power to be used for his will—for good. The young man needs to be told about his power and shown how to use it well. If he isn't told, as he finds out about it (and he inevitably will), he will experiment with it to see what he can do (and he can do a lot). He will try to pull apart families and friends; he will try to control others; he will try to destroy gods in his life and the lives of others. But who should have to go through that much trial and error to learn what generations of men have lived to learn? God uses progress. Young men are never too young to be told about the power they have. Show men how to use it and show men that they are constantly getting more. Demonstrate it in your life. Allow them to make mistakes and learn from them, and they will. Determine what can and can't be risked, but show them that they are entitled to a few mistakes. I know I am.

1

GETTING READY

K ITTY PUT DOWN HER READING and turned to me. "Jim, it says here that fathers should take their sons out on a weekend camping trip before they reach adolescence and prepare them for the feelings and changes that are coming. I think that is a good idea. Are you going to do that with our boys?"

Our eldest son Jamie was just reaching first grade, and Rami (rhymes with Jamie) was barely four, so I confess to having given very little thought to the topic. The idea had several advantages—a good father-and-son adventure, a chance to go camping, a rite of passage into adolescence, plus it had the endorsement of whatever important person she was reading this time. If I had been less involved in finding chords on the guitar, perhaps the author's name might have stuck with me. Over the years many people have complimented us on this great idea and we have never known who should get the credit.

Just when it happened no one knows, but the father-and-son trip before entering junior high became a family expectation like birthdays or summer vacations. We did not consciously think of it as a rite of passage into manhood at first. One brother might say to the other, "Where do you want to go on your trip with Dad—the mountains or the beach?"

"I don't know, I kinda like Owl Canyon."

"But that is the desert and the trip is in summer."

It was fun to be in on the excitement. Like many fathers, I often feel left out and wonder, "What are fathers for anyway?" My trouble started early in my role as a father. Jamie objected loud and long to being cared for by me. I lacked the facilities to render the liquid refreshment that he desired. This left me out of the action.

Even when he was older, force of habit would take him right past me to Mommy when his shirt needed buttoning. Even my calling out, "Here, let me help you with that" seemed to get lost in space. I would think to myself, "There must be a better way to be a dad."

Sure, mommies are important, but what are daddies for anyway? Maybe daddies are for throwing children in the air and catching them. Everyone liked that game, so until the boys grew too heavy to lift, I was at my zenith. I have never been as popular before or since that time. I loved it whenever the excitement about the trip with Dad brought me back into the action.

From time to time Jamie would come up to me and say things like, "Are you going to tell me about why teenagers act so dumb when we go on our trip?"

"Sure! I'll make a note to myself," I'd reply.

"Could you tell me a little about it now?" Jamie would add, leaning against my chest and looking wistful.

"What dumb things need explaining?" I would ask, and so we'd talk.

Rami was quite different about finding things out early. When sexual topics came up, he would frequently say, "I don't know about those things, but Dad will tell me on the trip." He would then trot off to jump over the furniture or bounce something off the wall. "Wait and find out" was his motto.

By letting Rami wait for answers, we were protecting his sexuality before he knew he was sexual. Children are born as sexual beings. It doesn't suddenly appear at thirteen. Answering Jamie's questions and letting Rami wait let each boy develop at his own pace.

As the date for the trip got closer, I began to tell friends about our plans. Their reactions surprised me. Most of my friends are counselors and almost all of them reacted by expecting me to be quite nervous about the experience, yet my feelings were of anticipation. If there was anything to worry about, it was forgetting some essential bit of camping gear.

The other expectation I encountered about the trip was also off base. Quite a few friends thought we were just now telling Jamie about the "birds and the bees." This was not the case. We had been answering questions and instructing both boys in the basics of sex as was appropriate to their ages. In addition, Jamie was there when his brother was born, so he never had questions about "where babies came from." When he saw Rami, his eyes popped open wide, but we thus had some of the essentials of sex education out of the way by the time he was two. Perhaps it is the idea of trying to tell children everything about sex at one time that makes people so nervous. We hoped we had found a better way.

What we were anticipating on our trip was something more complex than biology lessons, although some of those were in order. We were preparing a rite of passage into manhood with attention to all it meant to be an adolescent man. This meant (1) all those sudden emotions and reactions and how to deal with them; (2) dealing with peers, drugs, music, and such; (3) relating to girls; (4) teen-parent relationships; (5) biological changes of adolescence; and yes, (6) sexual biology and behavior.

Both Jamie and I set to work preparing our own list of topics that we wanted to cover on the trip. We also prepared check-off lists for equipment and daily menus. We were organized.

Kitty entertained doubts and questions about my list. What effect was this trip going to have? Was her dear husband up to handling these topics? She was to be left out of the talks and that made her skittish.

"What are you going to tell Jamie about my overprotectiveness?" she asked one night in bed. (Kitty has this habit of asking me difficult questions just as I am falling asleep.) "You know I won't be able to sleep while he is out on a date," she said woefully. "I don't want us to fight about curfews, and I want him to tell us where he is going."

"I don't know, but I'll make a note to myself," I said, hoping that would do it. Kitty however had other plans. For a while each time I grew drowsy my list grew a bit longer.

Jamie, for his part, did not know that this trip was unusual. He talked to his friends as though this was a universal experience for all children. He seemed to be puzzled whenever he had to explain what he meant by what he called "the father-and-son trip to learn about puberty." However, he did not dwell on it because there was some other reason for bringing up the topic with his friends.

Don't get the impression that our family life only consisted of preparing my sons to be men. This is not true. I just wanted to be a good dad. Harvests don't just appear in fields. Teachers and preachers don't spontaneously turn up with something meaningful to say. Dads don't suddenly become good dads and have great trips with their boys—at least I didn't. I worked at becoming a dad just as my sons would soon work at becoming men. Each stage of a man's life has its own work, a process which I describe in depth in my book *Life Passages for Men*.

I had given becoming a good dad some thought and decided on four goals. (They crept up on me actually.) I was holding my very own baby boy when the first thought struck. I knew then that I did not want to be mean to him. "Let me be a kind father," I whispered.

Later as the little boy held on to my pant leg and pulled

himself up, the second goal became clear. I wanted to be approachable. It would not be just wobbly legs that would need help to stay steady.

Busy days at work and graduate school produced the third goal. I wanted to stay involved with my children and not drift away into work. I wanted my boys to learn from me, so I had to get close to them.

By the time we had two boys, I wanted to raise two men—and Christian men at that. Two sons who would give manhood a good name became my fourth goal.

Fortunately Kitty and I worked on my first goal together. She liked the idea of my being kind to her babies, and she wanted them to like me. In her dreams they would be happy to see me come home and greet me at the door with kisses. That never happened, but by sharing the discipline, we escaped the "wait until your father gets home" pattern. This improved the chances that my boys would not think I was mean.

Discipline took time. We did not get results on the spot. It took repetition to teach the children anything. We didn't expect them to learn on the very first try when we taught them about their eyes, nose, ears, and toes. It was even more important to repeat discipline many times, since we were trying to change a little human being's natural inclination.

I watched other fathers and noticed that some of them gave their children whatever they wanted. These children were not afraid of their fathers, but I was afraid of the children. They were little monsters. Other fathers freely said no. "Don't do this." "Stop doing that." Their families liked it better when Dad was on safari. I thought, "There must be a better way."

Then I hit on a plan of giving the boys options whenever possible. "Just say no" might be a good way to handle the question of using drugs, but it is an unsatisfactory definition of fathering. You see, I wanted it all: both to be liked by my sons and to have well behaved boys.

Rather than saying no, I try to provide an improved alternative, and helping the boys to think through alternatives for themselves is better yet. Not only do they learn the skills of making choices but there is no need to rebel against something they have chosen themselves.

Of course, coming up with options takes more time than just saying no. Letting them make choices means living with more mistakes. Still, they are living with the mistakes I make as a dad, so it seems fair to let them make some. It is all part of finding a better way.

One Saturday morning Rami came into the bathroom as I was applying some motivational strategies to the shower head.

"Dad," he said, "can we get a basketball hoop?"

"We'll see," I answered.

"Good!" he said, much to my surprise. "When you say, 'We'll see,' it usually happens." With that he ran off.

When the surprise wore off, a satisfied feeling started to trickle into my soul. My son now expected me to try to make things work and find alternatives. I hadn't turned out mean. Maybe there was a better way after all.

The second of my four goals was to be approachable. I wanted my boys to be able to relate playfully with me. Humor seemed the best possible way, so I looked for ways we could laugh together. My tendency is to leave being serious about anything to the last resort anyway. Kitty tends to be much more careful. As a result, she is serious about being sure the family has fun, while I am lighthearted about the serious aspects of life.

I like to tease, so if the boys found something to tease me about, I knew we would be in business. As little fellows, they found it hard to see anything imperfect about me. With a little help they found the first imperfection right on the top of my head. Soon they added more of my quirks to the list.

I can still see the boys rolling on the sofa laughing at the idea that, not only did I not know how to program a computer by second grade, I had never even heard of one! Who said all dinosaurs are fossilized?

"And you didn't even know how to play Pac Man!" They

howled with laughter. (They had figured out the Pac Man business on their own.)

Joining in the laughter, I settled into a living room chair. The cat jumped into my lap; it didn't seem to mind having its ears scratched by an anachronism. Moments later the boys struck again.

"Hey, Dad! Tell us more about the days when you had hair! What else did you have back then?"

"Do either of you boys know what a slide rule is? That is what we used in the days before there were calculators."

"You mean like this?" said Rami, pointing to the calculator on his watch. The looks of disbelief gave way to flurries of laughter. At the price of my feeling a bit like a relic, we were having a good time. The boys had me on the run and took full advantage. Somehow I had not expected it to go this far until I was a grandfather. I only wanted to be a good dad.

The third goal I set for myself was to stay involved with my children. I had the trip to look forward to, but I wanted to be needed sooner than that. One crucial issue provided the excuse for a short trip—the boys needed to know how to protect themselves from child abuse before they could stay overnight with friends.

We took an afternoon trip to the park to throw some fris-bees and talk. It was an interesting park—the same one they park all the floats in after each Rose Bowl Parade. Since our visit was not near New Year's Day, the park was mostly deserted.

Explaining physical abuse to my sons went well. We all felt sad together about the mean things people do. Sexual abuse was different. They said right away that they didn't want to hear about that disgusting stuff. That meant that they already knew enough from some source to know they didn't like it.

When we tired of frisbees, we sat on a little hill in the sun-shine and talked about sexual abuse. I explained that people, both men and women, familiar and strangers, sometimes try to touch children in their private areas. I said that sometimes these abusers want the children to touch the adults in their private areas, and both of these were wrong. "These things should never happen to children, but sometimes they do."

"Why do people do that?" Rami wanted to know.

"Because some adults have not learned that it is their job to protect children, and some are bad people who like to hurt others," I said.

"Why do they like to do such yucky things?" Rami persisted.

"They think it is exciting and feels good. Many times they just like to have power and make other people do what they tell them to do. You know, like the bad guys on the cartoons that want to have all the power or rule the universe?"

"I don't want to talk about this stuff anymore," said Rami.

"Well, I don't like to talk about it either, but before we stop can you tell me what to do if someone tries to touch you in a private place?"

"Punch them in the nose and kick them and run as fast as you can," said Rami, jumping up to demonstrate how it would be done.

"Shout no, run away, and tell you," Jamie piped up, remembering what they taught him at school. Meanwhile, Rami was making mincemeat of the imaginary assailant.

"What if it happened at one of your friend's houses, Rami?" I asked.

Without slowing down a blow he replied, "I'd say stop and call you right away or run out of the house."

From there we made up a lot of "what if's," while throwing the frisbee and walking home. Some were serious: "What would you do if someone you didn't know said that we had told them to pick you up from school?" Some were humorous: "What would you do if a blob of Jello slimed its way over the hill and asked to play frisbee?" The humor helped relieve tension and keep their attention.

We had managed to discuss a difficult topic and get closer to each other. Talking isn't always comfortable, but I wanted to be a good dad.

Goal number four was to raise our boys to be men. That

brings us back to what this story is all about. Since I wanted to raise men, I had to learn how to foster the boys' sexuality.

Perhaps, before we get too far, it is time to define what I mean by sexuality. Sexuality is our total "maleness" or "female-ness" that we take with us in all our life experiences and inter-actions with others. It is composed of gender identity, sexual biology and response patterns, attitudes, experiences, and val-ues. Sex is an activity. Sexuality is how to be with oneself and others as a sexual person.

What I mean becomes clearer when we contrast the family's role in both sex and sexuality. Sexual experiences should never involve relatives, as that would be an extreme betrayal of trust and be very damaging. On the other hand, sexuality needs to be learned from one's family. We need to learn how to be fully male or female without being sexual.

It upsets me that in this culture my children will be pre-maturely sexualized—whether I like it or not. I can only reduce the degree of sexualization where possible. The most obvious ways are to behave nonsexually toward them myself and reduce their exposure to media material: TV, magazines, or movies that portray and arouse sexual feelings. On the other hand, I must actively expose them to material designed to educate and make them comfortable with their sexuality. I want to be one step ahead of their experiences so that they will learn healthy and godly ways, even if they must learn these lessons earlier than I would wish.

Besides protecting our children's sexuality, we had to help this delicate treasure to grow through support and encourage-ment. Kitty was in on this as well. In third grade Rami asked his mother, while she was tucking him into bed, if their good-night kiss was incest or not. That created a little tension! By talking it over with him in her reassuring way, she helped him sort out affection from sex.

The word *incest* didn't enter my vocabulary until graduate school. In fourth grade I felt there was something wrong with the affection I had for my adopted cousin. That led to some whispered discussions with peers about who could marry whom. Rami's question showed me how different my son's exposure to sex was from mine. So, whenever I would stop to think that I was raising two future men, it was reassuring to remember that we had a trip set aside to talk about some serious "men stuff."

———◆◆◆———

As the summer before junior high arrived for Jamie, we started to have serious discussions about the best destination for our three day adventure. The final destination we chose was a small uninhabited island off the coast of California called Anacapa. The U.S. Park service ran a small campground on the island that could accommodate up to thirty people. Conditions were primitive. Campers had to bring their own water and everything else they needed for their stay. All trash had to be "packed out" when one left. Since we were planning a backpack trip in the High Sierras later that summer, this trip would double as a training ground as well.

2

ON THE WAY

———◆◆◆———

THE DAY ARRIVED AT LAST. With almost everything packed in the car the night before, we kissed Mom good-bye and headed out early. After driving for an hour and chatting about the scenery, we stopped for breakfast. The restaurant had a huge metal tube full of holes set up by the road to lure travelers. We joked about the nasty sort of termites they must have in this place.

Over breakfast our first serious topic was launched. It was, in my mind, one of the two major points of the trip. You could describe the two points as (1) being a friend to yourself and (2) being a friend to women. If Jamie could get a good hold on these two parts of puberty and adult life, we would be off to a good start. We started our morning's discussion with how to be a friend to yourself during the changes of puberty. After the waitress took our order, I laid out some groundwork.

"Jamie, what changes happen in a boy's body during puberty?" He had already taken some health classes and had his own powers of observation as well.

He launched into a description. "What's that thing in your throat? You know, the lumpy thing here," he said, pointing to the front of his throat.

"Your Adam's apple."

"Yeah! Well, it gets bigger and starts to stick out and you get hair on your body."

"Remember when you were a little boy and you used to call it fur?"

"I wondered why you had fur all over your body but no hair on your head, Dad," he said with a grin. "Oh, and your voice gets low."

"That goes with the bigger Adam's apple," I said, ignoring the crack about the hair except for a smile. "Inside that lump, as you call it, are the vocal cords. As they get bigger, your voice gets lower. Sometimes in between there is a phase where nothing works right and the old voice gets squeaky. Singing and even talking can be embarrassing."

"Like Stephen."

"Exactly! I have a tape of one of my friends and me trying to sing at that age. Very funny stuff." He had the concept down.

"You mentioned hair growth. Where all does it grow?"

"On your arms, your face, down here, and on your chest."

"You are right, but it doesn't grow all those places at the same time. Usually your pubic hair and the hair under your arms grow first."

"Oh yeah! Under your arms."

"When your mom and I got married, I only had twelve hairs on my chest. The rest grew later. Your mom likes to tease me about that.

"I also remember that when I was about thirteen years old, I was quite interested in the progress being made by the fuzz on my upper lip. Somewhere I heard that if you shave, your mustache will grow in quicker. I read recently that this is not true, but since I didn't know any better, I got my dad's razor and shaved my lip. It was one of those silver-handled razors with doors that opened up when you turned the handle. Inside was a single blue blade. Very impressive! While I was at it I shaved my arm pits too. I can't remember why."

"You're weird!" said my son.

"Lucky for you! Now I have lots of stories.

"Anyway, what I found out was that my lip fuzz took a long time to grow back to how it had been before I shaved. The worst of it though was how prickly it felt under my arms while that hair grew back. I was really sorry for shaving there. I don't know how ladies do it.

"Did I ever tell you how I learned that ladies grew hair under their arms?" I continued.

"I don't think so."

"In sixth grade there was a girl who sat in front of me in class. I was a terrible speller, so whenever I needed to spell a word I would ask her.

"One day she wore a sundress without sleeves. She completely ignored me when I asked her how to spell a word. I looked up and saw the hair poking out from under her arm and gave it a little tug to get her attention."

"Dad!"

"It got her attention all right! She let out such a scream! Miss Clarabelle, our teacher, was furious. She took me in the storage room for three swats on the hand with a ruler and strict instructions that I was *never* to do that again. After that, I had to look up the word *scissors* in a dictionary and write it on the board five hundred times."

The waitress showed up with my decaffeinated coffee.

"You come from two families that have quite a bit of body hair, so you will probably be a fur ball yourself. Body hair is not altogether useless since it serves in places as a natural lubricant to keep your skin from rubbing off. Underarm hair works like that.

"Thanks to your Uncle Tim I took a terrible teasing from my friends about some hair that grew in the most useless of places, sort of in the middle of where one might sit down. I complained about it once to your uncle, and he told the boys at youth group, who never let me forget it."

"Why does hair grow there?"

"That's on my list of things to ask God when I have the chance."

Jamie was left to puzzle over these complications to puberty by the arrival of our food. Our waitress was a walking stereotype of the truck-stop waitress of middle America.

"More coffee, Honey?" she asked, whizzing up with her stainless steel coffeepot with the black handle. "Oh, you have decaf!" The annoyance was barely hidden in her tone. The coffeepot never stopped. It just rose and circled off like a plane that missed the landing strip and was going to go around for another try. This time it didn't come around again until we were about ready to leave.

"This orange juice is not fresh-squeezed," Jamie announced. "I like fresh-squeezed better."

"Do you have any idea why your body starts to change at puberty?" I asked. He didn't. We talked endocrine system while we ate. The role of that unique piece of brain called the *hypothalamus* was first on our list. There was no real need to mention this brain structure by name so I didn't.

"No one seems certain what part of your body decides to start puberty, but we know there is a special system of blood vessels that carry some chemicals from the brain to the pituitary gland. This happens about two years before you start to notice puberty is here. After that, the pituitary gland begins to make its gonadotropic hormones. GTH we call them because in America we feel smarter if we use letters rather than words.

"GTH," I explained, "are behind much of the mischief of puberty. They inspire the testes for boys or ovaries in girls to start secreting sex hormones. These hormonal changes lead to other symptoms like swelling and sensitivity in the nipples."

"For boys too?" Jamie interrupted, his eyes protruding a bit.

"Yes, boys too! And, there is increased sensitivity to pain in the testes."

"Like when you were showing me how to throw a baseball better and I didn't think that you would really throw it?" he asked.

"Exactly! I'm really sorry about that too!" I said with remorse and embarrassment. It took a moment to regroup. "Let's see. Oh, yes! Hormones also increase muscle development and your growth rate."

He flexed a muscle. "I'll look really buff!"

I smiled as my mind went back to the bowl of fresh spinach leaves his mother used to keep in the refrigerator for a little guy in his Batman cape to eat for strength when a bad guy needed to be subdued. (So he was mixing Batman and Popeye—he was eating his greens, wasn't he?)

"See that muscle?" he said.

A quick look produced no real evidence, so I said instead, "Let me feel that," and there was a nice hard spot in there. "Very fine!" I said, and he was pleased.

"There is one thing about hormone changes you might not like quite so well. Puberty thickens the skin, creating skin problems like acne."

"Do you think I'll have any?"

"I'm afraid so." His muscles were forgotten as he thought this over. Some acne was practically guaranteed for this poor boy. Treatment for acne has greatly improved in the last generation; still this formed in Jamie's mind one of the less blessed marks of promotion to puberty.

"Not everyone progresses through puberty at the same speed or in quite the same order. You can expect to seem different from others most of the time. That is pretty normal. If you have any concerns about your progress though, we will check it out for you to be sure everything is all right—you know, just like we did when your brother's teeth didn't grow in as soon as we expected."

Jamie nodded. "Do you think we should take these things of jelly with us for camping?" he asked. He seemed as reassured as he needed to be, and his mind was on to our adventure. "Let's pay the bill and go!"

Many of the things we talked about might seem rather trivial and possibly embarrassing. That is what puberty is like—there are many trivial things to cause us to be embarrassed and wonder if we are normal. How was I going to encourage my son to be open with me about the things that bothered him if I couldn't give him examples from my life? Now that he knew that I was "weird," it might not be so bad to appear a little "weird" himself. That is how we go about being friends to ourselves—by accepting those little wrinkles in our development.

———◆◆◆———

As we drove toward the boat-landing our conversation returned to the day's itinerary. Already we were feeling the excitement of the trip. We relaxed when we finally arrived and exchanged our reservations for tickets. From here on out it was smooth sailing.

Next to the landing was the Channel Islands Park Museum with exhibits of the various life forms, which we visited. The staff explained to us that this time of year the island was full of fledgling gulls who were just about able to fly. The unique Coreopsis flowers, which grow only on these islands, were already past their bloom, but a killer whale had been spotted near there—which was rather rare. Perhaps we might get a glimpse of that leviathan.

It was a cool sunny morning with the usual California haze when the call came to board the Island Fox for Anacapa. We were glad that we had already eaten our breakfast because the seas were calm (no danger of losing our meal) and the galley, which the advertising claimed would be serving breakfast on the trip, was closed. This created some grumbling and malcontents among the passengers. Most of those on board were out for a day trip and would return on the two o'clock boat. Four of us would be staying as campers.

During the crossing, we found out that the Santa Barbara Channel was a parking lot for currently unused oil drilling platforms. Since oil prices were down, we passed a long string of mammoth, awkward looking towers and the huge sledlike ships that are used to transport them from place to place. Even out here in the ocean these cities on stilts looked very imposing as the Island Fox slipped by hundreds of feet below their steel peaks.

Summer or not, it felt good to have our jackets on and feel the sun on our faces as we sat on the upper deck straining to get a view of something of interest. Jamie pulled his head inside his coat for a minute and then regained his interest in looking around. Just then a flying fish took off from the bow of the boat.

"Did you see that flying fish?" he said excitedly. "I just prayed that I would see something interesting and there was the fish!"

"Great!" I said, "Pray again!"

"Do you remember when we were in Minnesota fishing and Rami prayed to catch a fish and right away he got a bite?"

"Yes, I do, Jamie."

"Sometimes God gives me just what I ask for," Jamie said, peering seriously over the side of the boat, "and other times he doesn't. I don't know until I ask."

It was not too long after that when we caught the first glimpse of the light from the Anacapa lighthouse flashing through the haze. Soon after that the island's outline came into view. The shape of the island was long and low, as though someone with a giant lawnmower had come along and nipped the top off flat. To the north was Santa Cruz Island across a small strait. With its mountainous profile it managed to look like an island is supposed to look. Anacapa seemed to resemble a huge rock.

Anacapa actually comprises three islands and assorted rocks. Our boat approached the break between two of them and the pilot explained over his PA system about the brown pelicans that nested and flew around there and about the old French hermit who had given the spot its name—Frenchy's Cove. Through the clear water, we could watch schools of fish swimming below us as we cruised along the middle island.

Suddenly the boat veered off its course, put on speed, and headed out to sea again. Within ten minutes we were in the midst of two pods of bottle-nosed dolphins. For twenty minutes we cruised among what must have been sixty to eighty dolphins. It was like watching Jacques Cousteau except that these dolphins and their babies were swimming six or eight feet from where we stood peering over the bow. Every few seconds one would swim a few feet farther from the boat and jump up out of the water almost to our eye level. When the skipper put on the power to return to land, one dolphin still stayed in front of us before disappearing deep into the channel.

At the island anchorage we had lots to do, watching the crew hand-feed gulls or listening to the amazing rustle of whole schools of fish jumping out of the water at once. Campers were to be the last ones off the boat since we would stay longer, so there was no rush. Since the next step was to carry our packs and five gallons of water up one hundred fifty-three steps, I wasn't exactly in a hurry.

The peace of the place was interrupted every thirty seconds or so when the island "blew its nose." A loud, low, dissonant honk lingered over the water and cliffs each time the light-house foghorn sounded. At first we hoped that as the haze disappeared the island's congestion would clear up and the noise would stop, but that never happened during our three days. The noise carried well to every part of that flat rock of an island, but before we had sweated our way to the top of one hundred fifty-three steps, we were already learning to ignore the sound.

We left our skin-diving equipment at the landing, where the rangers assured us nothing had ever been stolen. We were easily convinced to leave lead weight belts at the bottom of the stairs!

From the top of the stairs, a short walk brought us in sight of the whole island. In the middle were four Spanish-style buildings that housed the rangers and island information center. A quarter mile away were a couple of outhouses and tents marking our destination. For a few moments I wondered if this had been such a good idea after all.

The trail wandered among the ice plant and dried grass. Signs proclaimed that we were to stay on the trails at all times.

Every once in a while there was a bench which Jamie headed for without comment. The 2.5 gallons of water in each of my hands convinced me to not question his guidance.

The campsite itself consisted of a small area of bumpy, grassy land with some picnic benches surrounded by railroad ties. The camp was in a hollow, crisscrossed by two trails. From here the island did not appear nearly so flat. The lighthouse lay to the east below us. Over a small rise to the north was the Pacific Ocean and the California coast. The west end of the rock was hidden from view over a small hill. To the south the island reached its maximum elevation, where a one-foot-wide trail led to a lonely bench sitting on top of a cliff. That looked like a good spot to explore, but first we would set up camp.

No human beings were around to watch us find a fairly smooth bump to set up our tent. Lots of gulls watched us eat the granola bars and sandwiches we had prepared for this moment. Just then, a ranger with all our boatmates in tow came through camp explaining the wonders of nature, including the two tiny buildings next to camp. These structures along with the picnic benches seemed to attract more attention than the three species of cactus which thought of this outpost as home.

Remembering that everything "packed in" had to be "packed out," we took care to put all our trash in a bag. Keeping this trash in order proved harder than we thought because of the wind that was constantly blowing, usually from the west, and the help of two intrepid, tenacious gulls. We watched the bird bandits on their raids. Gull bills seem to be more effective than camp knives for opening anything in reach. Garbage was their specialty. These two shredded trash and the wind spread it. Fortunately for us, we learned about their skills from seeing what the gulls we named Bonnie and Clyde had done to our neighbor's hoard of trash. After that, we kept all our trash in one tin can inside the little fire pit grill where no beak could reach.

The gull calls were constant from morning to night. Unlike

the foghorn that stayed awake all night, gull singing was constant only during daylight. Gulls, it appears, are only sociable within limits. Aside from Bonnie and Clyde, whose limits included our camp, most of the island was considered off-limits to humans or other birds by the local gull proprietors.

Everywhere one looked it seemed that two or three brown fledgling gulls were hurrying across the ice plant. They all had the appearance of children sneaking off with a cookie that they had surreptitiously garnered from the cookie jar. This gait was probably normal to them but unlike the proud defiance of the adult gulls, these teenagers seemed to be up to no good. We guessed they were smuggling something and feeling guilty.

The grass on the island hills was dry and brown. Jamie called it the "prairie in the ocean." These waving grasses were the reason that no open fires were allowed. We cooked on a little Primus stove and, although we had often enjoyed a campfire after dark at other camps, here we faced the reality that at nightfall we would go to bed without a fire. For the moment the sun hung pleasantly hot almost directly overhead.

3

MAKING CONNECTIONS
(Anacapa—Day 1)

A FTER LUNCH I COLLECTED FOUR DIAGRAMS and a camera. It was time for a walk. This was to be the classic sex education lecture. It was the moment that many parents spend a lifetime avoiding. My mind filled with the pictures of all the single-parent mothers who had brought their adolescent sons to my office so that they might hear from a stranger what their own vagrant fathers had failed to tell them. Strangely, those talks produced more nervousness for me than today's venture. I hoped it would not be too boring for Jamie. You can never tell what sort of reception Graafian follicles or bulbourethral glands are going to receive!

We took the trail up the hill to the highest point on the island. The walk took about two minutes. Below us, almost straight down, was the beach. There was even a park bench. Very civilized. We sat there for a while taking in our surroundings.

"Time to review some biology," I said, producing the diagrams. We started with the female reproductive system—side view.

"The fallopian tube looks like a claw," Jamie said after diligently studying the "map" for a while, "It is a kind of suction thingy." He laughed and continued, "The bladder looks like a lemon and the uterus like a banana. The ovary looks like an egg." In the cross section that is what they looked like.

"By strange coincidence, the ovary is where eggs are stored. There are millions there when a baby girl is born, but only about four hundred ever get ripened and used." We explored the functions of the various organs and tried to get them back into three-dimensional perspective.

Since there are many good books on how parents can give the biology lecture, I will only give the highlights of what we studied together. (You will find several of the better books on telling your children about sexual biology in the bibliography of this book.)

Various branches of the nervous system work together to control and provide sensation to the reproductive organs. "The main nerve down here," I said, pointing to the outer genitalia, "is called the *pudendal nerve.* Pudendal is a Latin word meaning 'shameful.' Early doctors did not think very highly of our sexual functions.

"Up here," I pointed to the vaginal and uteral areas, "the main nerve is the pelvic nerve. In addition this whole area is served by the two branches of the autonomic nervous system. Autonomic has the word *automatic* in it, and these nervous systems are that way—automatic. It is the same in men and women. That is why sexual responses seem to have a life of their own—apart from conscious control.

"With all these different nervous systems going you can see that the sexual response can be complicated. People, and perhaps women more so, respond differently to each sexual experience because of this complexity. This is why there is no one correct way to have sexual relations with someone. Your wife will be different each time. You will be different each time. You must let your body be your guide to what feels good and keep her informed as well. You need to be able to talk to each other as your feelings change. You know how sometimes getting your back rubbed can feel tickly, and other times the same thing will feel good?" Jamie nodded. "This is the same way."

Next we reviewed the slang names for women's body parts and explained the difference between pet names and slang names. "It is like the difference between calling someone names and calling them by their nickname, like 'Jamie.'"

Some may question the wisdom of such a discussion, but removing the mysterious aspect reduces the fascination with bad words. That is reason enough for me. This also provides a wonderful sense of privacy to the discussion that would not be there if he did his learning on the street first. Removing ignorance reduces anxiety about other topics as well.

The next diagram was the male reproductive system—side view. I pointed out that men had the same nerve branches as women—further, that erections require the combined effort of the nervous systems, the circulatory system and the muscles of the pelvic area.

"It is a complex process that will usually work right if you let it. Each man needs to learn his own sexual response at the same time that he teaches his body how he wants it to respond. It takes cooperation with yourself, time, and especially relaxation.

"Relaxing is a very important part of your sexual response. This is one extremely good reason to keep sexual activity inside marriage. You have lots of time to learn about your bodies. Like everything else, sex rarely works right the first few times you try.

"Some kids try to have sex in cars. They sneak around and try to avoid getting caught and that makes them anxious. When you are anxious you can't relax. Sometimes these kids teach their body to react the wrong way. Then they have a problem!"

"Can you fix it when you teach your body the wrong way?" Jamie wanted to know.

"Sure, but it isn't easy," I told him. "You can get sex therapy. There are lots of books that tell all about this stuff when you get to the age when you need to know about it."

Next we reviewed the slang names for male body parts. There seemed to be quite a few more than there were for women's parts.

From there we turned to fertilization. A simple diagram put the male and female side views together and showed the sperm and ovum pathways.

"How does the sperm get through without urine also coming through?" Jamie wanted to know.

"The prostate is the traffic control center for that. It is a valve for urine and a gland for making semen. It is also a pump for squirting the semen out of the penis.

"Lots of people confuse *prostate* with *prostrate,* which means to bow down. It makes for some funny sentences sometimes."

Jamie gave me a courtesy smile. He felt erie about this fertilization business. It just didn't seem right somehow for those body parts to be together like that. "It makes me feel strange in my stomach," he said at last.

As with the previous topics, we listed the slang words, this time for sexual activity. Later on he asked where I had found the diagrams to teach all these things. To that I replied that they came out of the textbook for my human sexuality class in college.

Fertilization wasn't the only thing to unnerve him. The diagrams of the male reproductive system led to a discussion of circumcision, which left a queasy feeling in his body as well.

"One thing that I forgot to mention was about penis sizes. There is a big deal made among men about penis sizes. They joke, brag, or hide if they feel inferior. It is one of the biggest deals about nothing that you will ever find.

"Regardless of the size of a man's penis when it is hanging limp (flaccid), they almost all turn out to be between five and seven inches long when erect. Being erect is different for different men; some still point downward, some point upwards. Some are straight and some bent. As long as you don't have one of the unusual problems that causes pain, they all work about the same. Just about any man and woman can match with a little creativity. All you really need to be sure is a decent physical exam. Ask the doctor to check anything unusual if you have doubts."

I explained birth control and conception by the fertilization diagram as well. Physical barriers to fertilization like the condom and diaphragm were shown to have clear functions. Then, we discussed chemical barriers like spermicidal foams, jellies, and creams. I described permanent barriers like vasectomies or tubal ligations. Finally, I showed Jamie how birth control pills block release of the ovum.

"Do you have any questions?" I asked.

"No," he said. "You just keep the sperm and the egg from touching." That was the heart of it.

"Christians do not agree about whether different types of birth control are according to what God wants for us," I told him. "That is another problem that you can study about in time. There are also practical and medical reasons to consider with different forms of birth control. When you are single, the best form of birth control is *don't have sex*. That one can be a problem for married people though."

The last diagram we looked at covered the menstrual cycle and was the most complex of all the pictures. I explained that the cycle began to run its course in young girls around twelve or thirteen with the first menstruation. This time is known as *menarche*. The last cycle is around age forty to fifty-five and this time is call *menopause*.

"Both of these times are responsible for great changes in women's bodies that are often reflected in the woman's feelings as well. Often these changes are accompanied by great emotional upset. Women go through these changes in a smaller way each month. For some women the changes don't amount to much but others can get very depressed or upset."

I explained menstruation itself and told of one neighbor who had first discovered menstruation when his wife started her period on their honeymoon. He was beside himself to find his wife "bleeding."

"So that is why Mom has those things in the bathroom," Jamie said, after taking a while to ponder the shock the neighbor had received. "I think it is better to know things ahead of time," he said, returning to the prior topic.

"Our bodies are full of surprises. It helps to know as much as we can. If you have questions about women, be sure to ask your mom. She will be glad you asked."

It was time for the afternoon boat to leave, so we headed off to the landing area to witness the great event. I was feeling satisfied with the trip so far.

———•◦•———

We took the rest of the afternoon to look around parts of the island. There would be time to cover lots of topics later, unless Jamie brought one up. This he did not do since there was much to fascinate the senses out here.

Supper presented the first major challenge of the trip. The objective was to heat a can of stew on the little white gas Primus stove. In case you don't know, this stove is round and will fit inside a one pound coffee can. It is basically a brass fuel tank with a burner on top surrounded by a metal wind screen that serves to hold a pan as well.

The stove we brought belonged to Jody, our pastor. He had demonstrated how to fill the tank with its liquid fuel. The trick, he said, was to heat the fuel inside the tank enough so that the physics of heat causing liquids to expand would make the fuel flow out of the top and fill a little ring that you then would light and presto—supper. "Purists," he said, "heat the fuel by holding the tank in their hands. I just light a match underneath." Seconds later his match produced a nice flow of fuel into the ring. Soon the little Primus was cherry red and roaring with a most satisfactory flame. That was in Jody's driveway.

Out here on a windswept rock it seemed that the fuel would evaporate almost as quickly as it came out of the tank, which was not very fast. I was deeply into my first container of matches before we heard the roar of the stove. That little thing could really generate the heat, and soon the stew was boiling.

The wind was not through with us, however, and before our plates were half empty, the stew was the same temperature as before it met the Primus roar. That was not very long because we were ravenous and the plates were soon clean.

Gauging that it was about a half hour to sunset, Jamie and I set off to the west end of the island to find the best view. We had not yet explored this way, so we allowed lots of time. Jamie pocketed a flashlight and we set off.

The trail out of camp led over a hill to a fork in the trail. The right hand fork appeared to lead to the west end so we went that way and were rewarded in about fifteen minutes by a magnificent view of the ocean, the sun, plus the middle and west parts of the Anacapa chain. This was a fine spot to tackle one of the less appealing parts of the next few years of my boy's life.

———◆◆◆———

"You know, Jamie, there is something I forgot to mention about the changes of puberty." Inwardly, I suspected that there was more I had forgotten but could not be sure just what it might be. Jamie looked up expectantly but said nothing. "Adolescence is a fabled time for feelings. They are often the same feelings you have now only more intense. If you are sad, you feel sadder. If you feel happy, you feel happier. It is like the difference between riding a merry-go-round and riding the loop trainer at an amusement park." (Jamie disdained the former and feared the latter, a human centrifuge.)

"Sometimes teens will go up and down and back and forth. Other times they will lock into emotions for a long time. Those periods with long lasting feelings are called moods. Moods can last for hours or sometimes days.

"It seems sometimes that these emotions are stronger during growth spurts, when your body is changing so fast that it can even be hard to feel coordinated."

"I don't think I like that," Jamie said. "Do you get over it very soon?" There were little vertical wrinkles between his eyebrows. He hardly ever got that scowl, so I guessed that this information was a little overwhelming to a boy who likes to feel in control of himself.

"Well, like everything else, some get it worse than others.

The worst of it is that these feelings or moods can sneak up on you, so that you don't notice what is happening. Once you see what is happening, your mind starts to feel better already. You can say, 'My! I'm in a mood today!' and already you are not so stuck. If you talk about your feelings with someone, you will find that you can live with whatever you feel. That is the funny thing about feelings, even the worst and strongest of them will go away if we pay close attention to what they are. When you do that, you will have gone a very long way to being an adult.

"Being realistic is one way to be reassured about feelings. It is not the most soothing way to reassure oneself, but it may be the most effective. In this case reassurance comes from understanding the problem and seeing the emotional cues that our actions are sending. In effect, our actions say to us, 'I can face this.' Sure, the feelings are scary, but if we do not run away there is the reassurance that these feelings are not, in the end, going to get the best of us."

Jamie said nothing, but the lines on his forehead were gone.

"You might end up with some of the same problems that your mom and I have—you lucky kid!"

"What is that?" he demanded.

"Well, it seems to be that if people can handle anger they can handle the rest of their emotions, because anger is one of the harder ones. When you were born, neither your mother nor I could handle anger very well. For your first few years you did not get very good training. Then we got some therapy, and we have improved quite a bit. I don't know how much good that has done for you.

"Neither your mom nor I like being angry, so we worked hard to pretend, even to ourselves, that we were not upset. We wouldn't yell, but if I was mad I'd stay away from the house or work in the garden, stuff like that. So when you came along and started having temper tantrums, we decided to teach you not to act that way. After that, instead of getting angry you would cry. There is nothing wrong with crying, but it works better being sad than mad. That is why in the last few years we have talked about how we want to act when we are angry in our house. That is why we had the practice times using words to describe how angry we were to each other. Rami has an easier time talking about anger, because by the time he was born we had already started to change.

"I'm still glad that no one at our house has temper tantrums, but I'm also glad we can talk about being irritated instead of doing angry things like calling names or staying away from each other. I still think, though, that you need more practice being angry out loud to make up for those first few years."

"I just don't remember to think about it when I am mad," Jamie said.

"I know," I said.

It was peaceful to sit together after that, remarking on our surroundings and speculating what Mom and Rami were doing about now. We both guessed that she would be reading him a book. It is a nice way to end a day.

"Look! There go five brown pelicans." We turned to watch the birds and the sunset. By now there were four other people at the island's end with us to watch the sunset. The sun seemed to split into horizontal slices of different colors as it reached the waves and began to sink rapidly into the Pacific. The wind suddenly seemed colder, so we zipped up our jackets.

On the way back to camp, we came across a very large bumblebee that flew like a hummingbird. It was in and out of flowers but took off when we got close. The next day a ranger told us what we saw *had* been a hummingbird—a very small species native to the island.

This end of the island was all gull rookery with the brown teenage sneaks in evidence all over the landscape. The skies were full of irate, screeching, diving, adult gulls. They always seemed to swoop in from our blind side and gave us quite a start as they skimmed our heads.

Jamie and I stayed close together and tried to look every direction at once. It was a no-win situation. If we watched the adults, then we would stumble upon the young. This would aggravate adult attacks immensely. If we watched for the young birds, the adults would sneak up on us more often. I began to marvel at the way these gulls had ignored the rangers earlier that day.

Jamie and I speculated about these things as we crawled into our sleeping bags. After squirming long enough to find a series of ridges in the ground that corresponded well with my back, I was ready to sleep. Before I drifted off, I took time to thank God for many things and remember the two family members at home. My heart was warm and joyful for the son beside me, the wonders of the Creator's world, and the comfort of God's love. There was love in the starry sky, my boy's eyes beside me, the thoughts about my wife, and even the beating of my heart against the bump of ground that was sticking me in the rib. God is good!

4

THE OWNER'S MANUAL
(Anacapa—Day 2)

———◆◆◆———

W HEN DAWN CAME NO ONE KNOWS, but the day was bright through the haze when we pulled our clothes inside the sleeping bag to warm them before dressing. The relentless wind continued to flap the sides of the tent. Through the tent door all we could see was waving grass and sky. The wind was stronger than it had been last night.

"What do you want for breakfast, Jamie?" The question was more polite than useful since we had planned the breakfast menu weeks ago, and there was little chance of appeal now.

"What have we got?"

"Oatmeal, Cream of Wheat for you, and hot chocolate. Why don't you find the packages and open them while I heat the water?"

This meant another round with that incendiary device. Remembering last night, I wondered if the three containers of matches we had would be enough for three days. Six matches later doubts were growing stronger. After warming the tank with matches, my hands and some temperate but warm verbal encouragement, we decided to forget the physics of the expansion of liquids with an increase in temperature and fill the little ring from the refill fuel tank. Soon our tin cups were full of warm cereal, and after a quick rinse we filled them with hot chocolate and turned our attention to the world around us. We found Bonnie and Clyde, the sea gulls, who—not being burdened with lighting stoves—were taking inventory of the camp.

The whole camping area was about one hundred feet square marked out by railroad ties. The two ladies who had come over on the boat with us had opted to sleep under the stars about thirty feet from us. One of them had crawled out of her sleeping bag and was attempting to convince the bird bandits that certain food stuffs were not for the taking. The gulls, for their part, had backed off five feet, but there they drew the line.

Washing dishes after breakfast amounted to swishing water around the cups with our fingers. Jamie proclaimed that this felt "sick," but it was quick.

The sun was already shining brightly when Jamie and I put on our sunscreen, and then pocketed our breakfast bars and lists of questions for the trip. Jamie found his Bible while I checked for the Bible study outline. The outline we were about to use was based on one prepared by Cliff and Joyce Penner,[1] but I modified it for the occasion. We headed off to the west end of the island. There were two trails heading that way, and the night before we had taken the right-hand turn. Now we could explore the left-hand fork.

A cool, brisk walk brought us to the west end, where we found a nice park bench and had the view all to ourselves. I had thought about having the Bible study on Sunday and the sex lecture today but didn't think it would do Jamie any good to study what the Bible says about sex until he knew what sex was. So Monday morning became the study time.

The first point on the outline affirmed that *sexuality is part of God's creation.* The Scripture passages were Genesis 1:26-28, Genesis 5:1-2, and Genesis 2:24-25. Jamie looked up and read the verses. We discussed each one.

It is rather important to know that God intended for there

to be sexual people and saw it was "very good." This implies a model of how people should be. Ideal people are endowed with sexuality, that is, maleness and femaleness. This beauty was tarnished by the Fall. By observing the rules that God gives us we should be able to be guided back toward the ideal. The Bible is an owner's manual, if you will, giving the specifications and operating limits for the best expression and appreciation of our sexual as well as social and spiritual selves. Operation outside of manufacturer's specifications voids the warranty and can cause extensive damage. Used as designed, sexuality is good stuff!

I used the analogy of a car while talking to Jamie. "Suppose I just got my first car and the owner's manual said to fill the tank with unleaded gas, but the station was a mile away. Since that long walk did not sound like fun, I found a garden hose and lots of water in my own yard that would work just fine to fill my tank. Why, I could even save money! How do you suppose that would work?"

"Not too good." (It was bad grammar, but this was not the time for that lesson.)

"When the father of one of my friends heard that I was getting married, he said to me in disgust, 'You don't have to own a cow to drink milk.' What do you suppose that means?"

"Does it mean that you don't have to get married for sexing?"

That gave me a chuckle. "Yes, but for some reason we call it having sex not sexing.

"Now, the owner's manual says to enjoy the wife of your youth and only drink the water from your own well. What do you suppose that means?"

"Only have sex with your own wife?" he said.

"Right! Now, suppose I wrapped the seat belt around my neck because it felt good and kept my neck from getting cold. Or, how about if I put oil in the tires or gas in the oil or air in the radiator? Would the car be very good?"

"It would be a piece of junk," he said.

"Even if it was a very good car to start with?" Jamie nodded in reply, so I continued, "Let's see what else the manufacturer says."

The second point on the outline stated that *the husband-wife (sexual) relationship symbolizes God's relationship with humanity* as shown in Ephesians 5:21-33 and Revelation 19:6-7.

Having our relationships in order is important for two reasons. First, healthy relationships are good for us. Second, they serve as an example to both ourselves and others of how God wants to treat us and how we treat God. Some people would say that the sexual union in marriage is the closest analogy we have to how our spirits become one with the Spirit of God. This seems to be Penner's point in relationship to the Ephesians passage that reads:

> Thus it is that (in the words of Scripture) "a man shall leave his father and mother and shall be joined to his wife, and the two shall become one flesh." It is a great truth that is hidden here. I for my part refer to Christ and the church, but it applies also individually: each of you must love his wife as his very self; and the woman must see to it that she pays her husband all respect. Ephesians 5:31-33

It is obvious that there are many more truths about marriage than could be included in one short teaching trip. My commitment to Jamie would take many more years to show him things like this marvelous model of how we need to change allegiance from our parents to Christ. In both marriage and salvation we need to "leave and join."

To Jamie this was like joining a team. An eleven-year-old can understand commitment and attachment in practical ways, but understanding abstract symbols is a mental ability that does not develop until around age thirteen. For this reason the exploration of symbols would have to wait a few years.

With an older child you could explain that Ephesians 5:31-33 implies that the sexual aspect of marriage carries part of the symbolic content of the relationship of the church to Christ. Notice that it does not give any mystical properties to the sexual activity itself. So many Scriptures are careful to keep sex and worship of God as far away from each other as possible that we need to be cautious. Here is part of the reason for such caution.

Most, if not all, of the Canaanite religions gave mystical properties to sexual activity, and made it part of their worship and fertility rites. Many current religions, including modern day American satanism, do the same. I think that this is part of the reason for the caution shown on this subject in the Scriptures. That is also one reason for the careful rules to protect one of God's more tarnished symbols—marriage.

While the Canaanites attributed positive magical powers to even the most hideous sexual activity, Martin Luther believed that even the best (marital sex) had bad properties and would cause God's Spirit to leave the room for three days. Both views are wrong because they give mystical, supernatural attributes where there are none. For human beings, sexual activity has a big impact, a truth that seems to be overlooked by many of those who are in search of the supernatural properties.

Now, while all of this makes a big difference to me, it would be lost on Jamie. He is too young to understand all the perversions of sexuality promoted as religious experiences. Instead, I stressed the theme of faithfulness—faithfulness to God and to keeping his symbols unspotted. This commitment is exactly what an eleven-year-old boy should learn.

"Someday, Jamie, you should be able to say to your children, 'Loving God and being a part of his church is just like your mother and me. We stick together. We love and respect one another. It is like being one person because even with our differences we do what is best for the other.' And your kids will say, 'We want to know God just like that.' Then you will have a warm glow inside that just won't quit."

Jamie smiled in anticipation. I hoped that he saw the same in his parents.

Our third topic was that the *biblical writers assume married couples enjoy sexual pleasure.* For this we looked at Song of Songs 1:1-4, Ecclesiastes 9:7-10, and 1 Corinthians 7:3-5.

In Song of Songs we found sexual pleasure for the woman described, while the Ecclesiastes passage recommends the same for the man (with the wife of his youth). First Corinthians is the well known passage about husbands and wives having claim to each other's bodies and mutual sexual satisfaction. Jamie took all this in stride and pretty much without comment except, "That seems fair."

The fourth point in our study was that the *barriers between sexes were broken down in Christ* as stated in Galatians 3:28.

It took a while for this to make much difference to Jamie. We had neglected his education in that we had never mentioned the "battle of the sexes" at home. The major difference between the sexes he knew of was that women could breastfeed and men could not. When he was four, he thought he had found another difference when he went to the bank with his mother to withdraw funds. Jamie asked her, "Why does Dad go to work for money, when you just have to go down to the bank and get some?"

Still, none of these things were barriers between the sexes, so Jamie received a short history lesson. He first had to understand that historically women have been second-class citizens on much of this planet. It was Jesus who made it clear that the things that some thought made one group more valuable than the other must not count with Christians. All people may enter equally into union with Christ.

Women at Jesus' time were considered such mental midgets that they could not even testify in court. In spite of this, Jesus first revealed that he was the Messiah to a woman. Women were also chosen as the first witnesses of the resurrection. That is what breaking down the barriers meant then. Now it means that we need to guard against any beliefs that women are less valuable than men.

Next we turned to the two points I had added to the Bible

study outline. The fifth point introduced the broad topic of *rules surrounding sex*. We examined two passages (Lv 20:1-21 and Sg 2:7).

"These are the safe operating limits for your new car," I told Jamie. "We won't study them all today but you will get a general idea. Some of the rules need to be adapted to new road conditions but the principles remain the same. For instance, read the first five verses of Leviticus 20." He did and looked puzzled.

I explained that Molech worship involved child sacrifices and possible sexual activity with children to insure good crops, among other things, for the people. In fact, some scholars believe that Molech may not have been a god but a ritual used for several gods.

For us this Scripture means that God, by virtue of the principles involved, would take a dim view of sacrificing children to promote economic prosperity or religion. He would also hate sexual abuse of children or allowing children to be involved in child pornography. We looked at Leviticus 19:29 to be sure. It seemed clear; parents should protect their children from sexual activity.

It is not just parents who are responsible for children. Neighbors are responsible for neighborhood children. It does not do to pretend that nothing happened. Verse four teaches that God would oppose any nation or people who would allow others to get away with these activities.

> If the common people connive at it when a man has given a child of his to Molech and do not put him to death, I will set my face against man and family, and both him and all who follow him in his wanton following after Molech, I will cut off from their people. Leviticus 20:4-5

Through the following verses, we also addressed incest. Verses 11-21 make this third rule clear. I explained that caring for family means no sex with relatives by blood or marriage.

Everyone deserves a chance to know that they are loved for themselves and not because they provide sexual gratification. So we have to have relatives who don't treat us sexually. If our family does not provide them, then our church family certainly must.

"I miss seeing my cousins," Jamie said presently. "We don't have any relatives out here."

"You had fun with them, didn't you?" I said. He nodded.

"When we go camping with the people from church it is like having brothers and sisters and cousins to play with," I said hopefully.

"I like my real cousins better," he said.

We went back to looking for rules and found that human sexuality was for other people only—no animals.

"That's disgusting!" Jamie said and turned away. "Do people really do those things?"

I pointed out to him that while bestiality, homosexuality, child prostitution, and adultery were part of numerous Canaanite and present-day religions, there were many people in America and elsewhere who did them simply because they could get away with it. Their god is whatever feels good to them.

"Even when we eliminate animals, we aren't to have sex with just any human being," I said, turning back to the text. "Sex between two men or two women is wrong also." Jamie nodded vigorously at this. Any boy going into junior high *should* know that one. Although with the practice of homosexuality being promoted as an alternate lifestyle, that is changing. We moved on.

Not exposing our nudity, or that of relatives, was the rule in verse 17. Jamie had no problem with this or the next one which summarizes them all—sex is reserved for marriage partners. He had already lived long enough to see what adultery had done to some of his friends' lives.

"Perversion," I told him, "is a word that means something good has been twisted into something bad. These nasty things we have been reading about are perversions. All these perversions can be avoided by worshiping the true God, and keeping sex for marriage. That is one way of loving your female neighbor as yourself."

The final rule came from Song of Songs. It contains a phrase that is repeated three times in that book. It reads, "Don't awaken love before its time."

"Sexual love and attraction are a powerful force," I told him. "It can help bring two people together as you will read sometime when you study the whole book. This love can make your life miserable if you wake it up before the right time. The things we see and do can awaken our desire before we have a way to handle the feelings. Did you ever get sleepy during school?"

"Oh, sure!" he said.

"Fighting desire is as miserable as getting very tired in the middle of the day and trying to stay awake. There is nothing wrong with feeling tired, but when it arrives before its time it can make us wish it had not!

"Solomon," I told Jamie, "eventually lost his kingdom because he did not keep his own advice. He ended up building temples to Molech and Astarte (also called Ashtoreth or Ishtar) and other gods on what was probably to become the Mount of Olives! Not a good move!"

With Leviticus 20:4-5 there was also more background information and application than what we discussed at the time. The Astarte fertility cult, for example, leaned heavily on temple prostitution for their rituals. One branch practiced sex with girls and women while the other, involving boys, was homosexual. Had we gone back a few verses in Leviticus we would have seen a powerful prohibition of these activities as well. It says with great emphasis that this is something that parents are not to do to their boys and girls.

Astarte was a favorite of the Philistines and Syrians. References to Astarte worship are scattered among well-known Bible stories. When King Saul was killed, his body was taken by the Philistines and placed in a temple of the female prostitutes. His head was taken to a temple of the male prostitutes. Every Philistine town of any consequence needed its own temples.

Soon after Solomon's reign the Palestine countryside was covered with what we politely translate *Ashtoreths*. These were carved wooden genitals that the prophets describe as being on every hill and under every tree. It is not so different right now. In an age of processed food we use wood pulp and printer's ink instead of wood to keep our Ashtoreths or pornography in our magazine racks and bathrooms. The perverse sexual rituals may be rented for your VCR as well.

Sometimes trying to think of our sexuality as a good thing after all this is like taking a flight after a major airline disaster; we are a little uneasy! (A few of us are terrified.) Jamie seemed ready to heed the warnings in the story of Solomon but was not too concerned.

We moved to the sixth and final point in our study: *following God is important.* This is the choice that each young man must make, and it is not without consequences. We studied God's promises in Deuteronomy 27:15 to 28:68. It took a while to read.

The entire nation of Israel was to review this Scripture every seven years. Every king had to make his own handwritten copy of the portion of God's law that includes this passage. My son was well over seven and had not yet heard the promised blessings and curses, so I was way behind schedule.

"Well," I said when at last Jamie finished the reading. "Do you think God is serious about whether we are obedient or not?"

"Wow!" said Jamie. Then he said the most amazing thing. "This is like that scary movie we saw at church on the tribulation."

This showed that the boy's mind was quite busy during those silences when I wondered if he was getting anything out of this at all, so I answered, "Yes. You can see these promises and curses spoken again in the Book of Revelation where we are told that we will be blessed if we read, listen, and obey." We talked of history and how the generation that crucified Jesus had illustrated God's seriousness on this matter for all time. Still, this called for commitment and obedience, and Jamie had not put his intentions into words, so I asked, "Whose side will you be on? Who will you obey?"

"God's side," he said. His eyes had a faraway look, but his jaw was set like he meant it.

We headed back to camp soon after that. As always, the walks around the island were spiced up by the sneaking of the adolescent gulls and the dive-bombing runs of their adult guardians. If we saw the young birds we could anticipate a buzz-bombing very quickly thereafter. It seemed strange that the island rangers rarely got buzzed. Could it be that the birds knew them? We could not tell.

5

STAYING ON COURSE
(Anacapa—Day 2)

———◆◆◆———

WHILE WATCHING THE GULLS fight in the air overhead, we noticed that they always attacked each other from behind. They always attacked us from behind as well. We began to joke that our caps were our beaks and this was why they also attacked us from behind. This led to an experiment. What if we turned our beaks around? We did and sure enough the gulls attacked us from the front.

Since the goal was to avoid attack altogether, Jamie set his "beak" on backward while mine went on forward. Now we had them! The next thing we knew, we were buzzed from the side. This was a new flight pattern. Apparently, the gulls were accepting a compromise position and making the best of things. Now the genius of the ranger hats with their round flat rims was apparent. No matter what angle the poor gulls selected for attack, there was a "beak" aimed right at them.

As we walked, Jamie took out his list and after checking for a bit, he asked: "What sort of things should you like about a girl? Who should you hang out with?" Later I noticed he had combined two questions. This suggested to me that the ideas about girls and those about friends were already moving closer together in his mind. He now saw these two questions as related even though they were numbers one and four on his list.

"Well, Jamie, what do you like about the friends that you have right now?"

"We have fun."

"You like doing things and talking together—that is important. What else?"

"Do you mean church friends or school friends?"

"Ah! Now, that is an important distinction. What is the difference between your school friends and church friends?"

"My school friends don't believe in Jesus and the Bible. Well, some of them don't. They don't go to youth group. All John does is watch TV. He won't even read."

"So your friends have different values," then, thinking the word *values* was too abstract, I added: "Different things are important to them. You spend your time differently. You believe differently. Some friends are Christians and others are not."

"One is a Buddhist," Jamie remembered.

"Do you still pray for him?"

"Sometimes, but he goes to a different school now."

"What does the saying 'you can tell a man by the company he keeps' mean?"

"Doesn't that mean that you'll act the way your friends do?"

"That is right. Do you act the way your friends do or do they act the way you do?"

"Sometimes."

"Great Grandpa Wilder had a saying: If you have one boy, you have a boy. If you have two boys, you have half a boy. If you have three boys, you have no boy at all. What does that mean?"

"With more boys you get in more trouble?" Jamie was not too sure on this one.

"So that is what it means! I always wondered!" Jamie

grinned, which made me drop my straight face. "Actually, he had noticed that when you get boys together they don't get much work done. You see, our friends have a big effect on us, and we should pick friends who will help us become the people we want to be. Does that make sense?"

Jamie nodded and I paused before going on. "On the other hand, we have an influence on our friends. We should have a few friends on whom we are being a good influence, but we should not have too many of them until we are quite strongly the person we want to be."

After a pause to let the mental pools of what I hoped was wisdom refill, I turned to the subset of friends known as girls. "Among your friends, there are usually some very special friends. These friends have a very big influence on you, and you need to choose them very carefully. You want to pick someone who believes like you do about all the important things. Among these friends are your special girlfriends. One close girlfriend can have more effect on you than ten boys.

"What kids don't usually realize is that most boys will date a lot of girls, but only a few of them become special sorts of girl-friends. Those special friends need to be very carefully selected because you will let them into the softest, most delicate parts of yourself where you keep your deepest values, fondest memories, and most precious dreams. If your friends are not trustworthy, they will slowly eat away and destroy your best parts through doubt, ridicule, and betrayal. That hurts a lot, while a good friend will help you to grow."

We stopped back in camp for a snack, then headed up to the concrete pad on the south shore. These breaks provided a change of pace and produced lots of junior-high kinds of comments about the little houses next to camp. With the restart of our walk and a little inquiry, Jamie produced his list again.

"What about drugs, alcohol, and smoking?" he asked. This was an excellent question that had been completely left off my list. It was a good thing that we had both brought our lists and not relied on mine alone.

"You know, I didn't even think of that question! Can you believe it?" Still, we had talked about these topics before, so I took them one at a time, asking what he knew and what else he wanted to know about that particular matter. Yes, I had tried a cigarette and nearly coughed my fool head off after a puff. We had even rolled a few of our own with wood shavings, tea, and tree leaves, always with the same or worse results. I even tried an uncle's pipe, only to find out that it does not taste at all like it smells.

My descriptions were met with peals of laughter. "You're dumb, Dad!"

"That is about right," I replied, wondering what was so interesting about being able to see my breath or blow out smoke. Then I made sure that he knew the health hazards of smoking, chewing, or snorting tobacco which, it turned out, he already did.

"Did you ever use drugs?" he asked presently.

"Not on purpose." There was the time my cousin and I had used the glue in the darkroom and gotten so buzzed that I fell down the stairway, and it didn't even hurt—until later. After that, we followed the instructions to "use in a well-ventilated area." No, I hadn't used other drugs, although many people I knew had been involved with drugs.

"I kind of like my brain! You know that I had a stroke when I was two years old and lost a piece of my brain, so I have had to live the rest of my life without having a whole brain. I'm not too eager to lose parts of the rest of it, permanently or temporarily. Still, I imagine this brings up a question in your mind."

"Yeah!" He knew what it was. "Why do you drink wine? You say that you don't like the way it tastes. You don't like the way coffee or tea taste and you drink them too. Why do you drink things you don't like?"

I think he was letting me off the hook. There were two issues here that shouldn't be confused although they had one aspect in common. First the easy one.

"I drink and eat quite a few things just to be sociable with

friends and relatives. I even drink coffee or tea at work to avoid
the boredom of drinking water all the time. Besides that, I
don't mind them all that much. I can hardly stand carbonated
beverages, so I almost never drink them." Still this left the
main topic untouched.

"Alcohol, though, is a drug and can be a dangerous one at
that. The reason that I started drinking wine was that I didn't
have any good reason to stop me. The Bible does not seem to
prohibit wine as far as I can tell. God says we should not get
drunk, and I knew that I didn't want to get drunk, so I never
have.

"I stop drinking when I can feel the effects of the alcohol.
Since I know that the body gets rid of about one drink each
hour, I try not to drink more than one drink an hour. I do this
when I'm with people who drink wine the way I do with
people who drink coffee. I don't drink over three cups of coffee or three glasses of wine because I don't like the way it
affects me. All together I drink about a glass of wine a month.
Now, depending on which study you read, that is either bad or
good for you.

"What I found out that has kept me from drinking any alcohol for the last half year or so is that even one drink will make
me feel tired the next day. Most of the time I want to have my
full level of energy, so it simply is not worth it to me to have
low energy. One of my friends found out that he didn't need
his morning coffee when he gave up his can of beer with
supper.

"I don't like the effects of caffeine either; that is why I drink
decaffeinated tea and coffee. Some people believe that God is
against all alcohol and all caffeine. Others read the same verses
and say differently. Everyone agrees that God is against getting
drunk or anything that makes us lose control of our judgment
or choices. All four of your grandparents disagree very strongly
with me as to what God commands about alcohol. In time you
will have to study the matter for yourself. I hope that you are
ready morally and spiritually by the time you have to choose in
real life, which will be a long time before you can choose

legally. And by the way, Son, we Christians are to obey the law.

"What I am doing is a calculated risk, like living in L.A., eating French fries (with our family's history of heart problems), driving a car, or taking a prescription painkiller. I'm not sure what I am doing is wise, because for some people it is certain death. That is also why I hardly ever eat French fries.

"I do have a rule that I won't break. If I ever think to myself, 'Boy, I could use a drink!' or 'A drink would help me relax,' then I absolutely won't have a drink. The same goes with caffeine. If I think, 'Some coffee would help me wake up,' then I won't drink any. I do not want to take chances with getting hooked on something. Does that make any sense?"

Jamie thought. "Yes," he said at last, "except for why you drink and eat things you don't like."

"Several reasons really. Sometimes it is accepting hospitality from others, like eating food with onions in it. Other times it is because the things I don't like are better than other choices that I like even less. For instance, I don't like 7-UP, but I like cola even less, so I'll pick 7-UP."

"But you had never even tasted Coke, so how do you know?" Jamie said impishly.

"You are right! It just looks brown and disgusting."

"I think it is great! Besides, you told us not to judge things before we try them." He drove home his advantage.

"You have got me there," I said.

"So why don't you try some?"

"If I have to choose between Coke and dying of thirst in the desert I would. It is all in the choice! Occasionally," I said, returning to the theme, "I pick something I don't like because the things I don't enjoy are good for me—like string beans. You know how that goes!"

Jamie made a face. "Let's do something," he said presently.

It was around 11:00 A.M., so we decided to take our first snorkeling trip. The day's boat load of tourists had arrived and the loading area would be free. The one hundred fifty-three stairs formed the only way up and down to the ocean for everyone but the birds. When we arrived, however, the entryway was closed off. We could hear banging, thuds, and splashes. On the cliffs below we could see forestry service workers dislodging loose rocks from the cliffs that then fell into the ocean below. This procedure, we were told, would last until the afternoon boat departure at which time we could swim. After watching rocks fall for awhile, we headed to the island information center to examine the exhibits and get a self-guiding nature trail booklet.

From there we followed the trail back to Cathedral Cove using a slightly different trail than we had used before. These small variations made walks more interesting. On an island this size there were limited new thrills unless one looked for small details, slight variations, and subtle patterns. There was always something interesting if we took the time to find and enjoy it. A good metaphor for marital sex, I thought, keeping my thoughts to myself.

"Got a topic to discuss while we walk, Jamie?"

"What about clothes and dressing up?"

"Ah! A simple, if expensive, topic! Most of us come up a quart low in the self-esteem department during teen years. Since our clothes have an effect on how people think about us, especially when you first meet, clothes can get to be very important for some people. It used to be very important only for girls, whose value was falsely based on how good they looked. In the last decade, the fashion industry has worked very hard and spent millions of dollars to convince boys and men that their value is also based on the name on their shoes or shirt. I think the message will be with us for a good long time. I mean, what is easier to do, buy self-esteem for $75.00 that you can wear on your feet, or wait until you can buy a car in order to impress others?

"I'm sure that you will want to use clothes from time to time to help you fit in with the group and feel good about yourself. Just don't rely on that one thing for all your self-esteem or acceptance. Ultimately it is not satisfying to be one of the herd and be led around by fashion designers or fads."

"What is a fad?"

"That is something of no real value or importance that seems very important or desirable at the time. Oh! And it usually costs money!"

"Like Town and Country Surf T-shirts?" Jamie added.

"That is the idea."

Meanwhile Jamie stopped to examine a gum plant that, according to our guide book, was called *Grindelia*. All the budding flowers looked like they had sprung a leak and oozed sap all over themselves. Gingerly, he touched the sap and found it quite solid, but slightly tacky, like glue that has almost set.

"How weird!" he said, pulling back. I waited for more but that phrase seemed to have captured the essence for him and now his interests moved on. "Can we have lunch now?" he said over his shoulder as he headed up the hill to camp.

The morning boat had brought seven more campers. There was a father with two teenage daughters and a son in one group, and a young couple in the other. The couple set up a tent of magnificence and splendor that dwarfed anything else in camp. For this the husband was quickly dubbed "Lawrence of Arabia." Warnings about Bonnie and Clyde were soon shared with the new arrivals, but both groups ended up learning by experience. It amounted to about an hour's worth of experience all together by the time they were through collecting their trash from an eighth mile semicircle downwind from camp.

6

YIELD?
(Anacapa—Day 2)

———◆◆◆———

LUNCH WAS A ZIP, or at least it was supposed to be. The peanut butter and honey sandwiches were already made and the carrots were pre-cut. All that remained was opening a can or two of sardines. When the tab broke off the can, this job suddenly got messy. It was a mess that attracted Bonnie (or was it Clyde?) to within a few feet of our table.

"These didn't come all the way from Norway just for you!" I scolded. The plucky bird just inched a bit closer. As soon as the can was in the garbage container under the fire grate, it appeared that someone had glued the bird to the top of the grate—for there it stayed, tugging at the can that wouldn't come out.

Our binoculars revealed that the ocean access was still roped off for us, so we took our newly acquired guidebook on a tour of the rock. Our first stop was to see the local varieties of cactus. Children seem always to be fascinated with cactus. This doesn't mean that they want to spend very long looking at cactus, but they like the potential that cactus represents. Now there is a little plant that can defend itself and with a vengeance!

No cactus in California can match the reputation of the cholla or "jumping cactus." Fabled in camping lore, the cholla can't really jump, but don't try to prove that to anyone since this little treasure can stick to anything that brushes against it, gaining it the scientific name of *Opuntia prolifera*, meaning "lots of stickers."

Jamie remembered and recounted several stories about cholla. He told of Lady, the boxer, a dog remembered for her gentleness and curiosity. She would walk the pads off her feet for the children, but not go near anything that even reminded her of the place where she had tried to scratch her way out of a patch of cholla as a puppy. He also recalled Cathy, who had tragically discovered the plant as a little girl on her way to a nice clam chowder meal and refused for years to eat clam chowder again because of the painful memory she then associated with it. So when we read in the guidebook "please remember to stay on the trails," we heartily agreed. As we headed down the path, I returned to the topics that had brought us to Anacapa. Just as Jamie remembered the stories about cholla and applied them to our hike when choosing where to walk, so telling him his family history would teach him how to walk through life. The central part of a boy's rite of passage is making him a part of history. Jamie's first step back into history would lead straight into my life story.

———•◆•———

"Would you like me to tell you about how I grew up and learned about sex and puberty?"

"Sure!" said Jamie, popping out of the reverie inspired by the cactus calamities. He stopped a step to let me catch up with him, his face expectant while I struggled with where to start. The idea seemed like a good one a few seconds before, but now appeared monumental. My dismay lifted with the appearance of a simple idea.

"I'll start at the beginning," I said, smiling down at my son. "I started learning about boys and girls by playing hospital in grade school. Five of us, two boys and three girls, played lots of different things together. One day we played hospital. That game included some physical exams. We gave in to our curiosity by looking and poking with our fingers. We knew these were the parts that made us different, but we didn't know they were supposed to feel good."

Jamie's eyes popped open. "You really did that when you were a kid, Dad?"

"Yes, I did. We were very nervous and scared because we knew somehow that we would be in trouble if someone caught us, so the game only lasted a few minutes. I know we felt guilty about it, because we never tried that game again.

"Then our family moved to a neighborhood where there were mostly girls. Most of my childhood was spent with girls as my most frequent playmates. We didn't always get along. There were some boy-girl standoffs, but they didn't last long. The girls either didn't know that there were such things as 'cooties,' or neglected to inform us, so we played well together. We liked to play house, cowboys and Indians, pirates, or act one of the many stories from the books we read. This formed in my mind a lasting association between girls and friendship. Now that I am a man I think of friendship with women the same way. Being friends is the first and most natural relationship between the sexes. As I got older, there were some romantic and sexual feelings to be added in but not if they interfered with the friendship.

"Many of our projects, like our games, were cooperative ones with pooled resources. We rarely had enough of anything to play alone. We wrote poems, built clubhouses, and got into mischief together. To this day I'd rather do projects with someone else."

Just then we cleared the top of the hill and stopped at a trail marker. It was an unlikely spot to find anything of interest, just a few rather boring-looking bushes, "Kitchen Midden," according to the guidebook. Strange name for a bush, I thought, but the book explained this was a garbage pile left by generations of Chumash Indians who had stopped to eat on this island. Sure enough! On closer examination, we were standing on a pile of broken seashells and bones. Suddenly, this drab bump in the road was quite interesting. We tried to imagine the scene and I suddenly felt very much like an intruder into someone else's history.

As we moved on past the old garbage dump, I continued the narrative. "My brother and I got into a discussion about dancing when I was in sixth grade and he was in fifth. I said that our parents were against dancing because touching shoulders in dancing had something to do with having babies. My brother thought that was ridiculous. Having babies was clearly related to a man and woman being in bed together where something would run back and forth between them. He wasn't sure just what."

This tickled Jamie no end. "You didn't know where babies came from in sixth grade?" He would be starting sixth grade at the end of this summer. He continued laughing. "You really thought that! I can't believe it!"

We were still chuckling when we arrived at the edge of the island, where our guidebook said we might see other islands like San Nicolas or the famous Santa Catalina Island some fifty miles away. We saw haze. Very nice haze to be sure, but haze all the same. I told Jamie of a previous trip when his mother and I had seen hundreds of sea lions "hauled out" on the beach below us.

"There aren't any now," Jamie announced and began to walk on. "Let's keep going."

It seems that the sea lions I could remember were no more interesting than the Chumash Indians we read about in the guidebook. The stories about growing up seemed to be catching his attention, however.

"I first learned the 'F' word from one of my friends who was rather a bully at times. Staying on his good side strongly reduced the chances that he would threaten to hit you 'where it counts' with his slingshot. He told me to say the words to 'Yankee Doodle,' but start each word with an 'F.' Towards the end he nearly fell in the creek laughing. I wanted to know what was so funny. He had me say it again and reacted the same way. Finally, he asked me if I didn't know the word, which as you can see I didn't. He told me it was a bad word but couldn't explain exactly why.

"I had recently taken a hard slap to the face from the missionary who ran our Christian school for saying, 'Well, I'll be a blue-nosed gopher!' I had been all the more surprised about the slap since I had learned the 'bad' expression from a Christian children's book. I decided to keep this new word in mind and take care not to say it to prevent any more assaults on my face. Fortunately the mnemonic device of the song helped me to remember the collection of sounds that made the new bad word."

Jamie thought this development over seriously. "Did you tell your parents when that teacher slapped you?"

"No," I said, "I was afraid that I would get in trouble. When I was a kid I thought that grownups were always right and that I must have done something wrong, so I didn't want my parents mad at me. Now I know that they would not have been angry at me. They wish I had told them about that and quite a few other things. The same missionary that slapped me was the one that left Uncle Tim black and blue for almost a month when he didn't get all his Bible verses memorized. We didn't tell them about that either."

"Here is the next marker," Jamie announced suddenly. Our guidebook said this stop was to "smell the local plants and listen to the flies and birds." This was not a major attraction, and we soon moved on.

"Jane was my best female friend for many years. When I became a teenager, she helped explain to me many of the secret interactions between boyfriends and girlfriends. She explained in depth about holding hands, French kissing, flirting, sending notes, and avoiding problems from parents. Although we spent quite a bit of time together and were often teased in adolescence by those who suspected that we had a romantic relationship, Jane and I continued as friends. It seemed natural to support each other in beginning romantic involvements with others because we had shared our other problems along the way."

It never occurred to us to even kiss each other, and though we remain friends to this day, we still wouldn't. It seems out of place to have to mention that we didn't even hold hands, but there seems to be a presumption that in becoming an adolescent, the relationship between sexes must be sexual. That is one reason we have so many problems and pressures.

"Sometimes," I continued, "it can be very helpful to get a girl's point of view when you are trying to develop social skills. It helped me a lot to have someone to talk with about my feelings."

Jamie thought for a minute. "I have a friend right now who is a neighbor that I play with quite a lot. She goes to the Sunday evening church club. I like playing with her and her brother quite a lot."

"Do you talk to her about girls?" I asked, aware that he did, but wondering if he had noticed what he was doing. A slightly embarrassed smile let me know the answer, but that was about all the response I received.

"Sometimes," he said.

After walking in silence for a bit, I went for the big story, my formal instruction from Dad about the "birds and the bees." Actually, it was later that I learned that this was called the "birds and the bees" talk since Dad either didn't know or didn't care. Consequently I still don't know if Dad was a bird or a bee. Dad said, "It is about time that you boys learned about sex." Just like that!

Almost everyone has a story. It seems to be a moment that is rarely forgotten by those who have received this rite of passage. Russell Baker, in *Growing Up*, tells this story about having his uncle explain sex to him.

> "Look here," he said, "you know how babies are made, don't you?"
> "Sure," I said.
> "Well, that's all there is to it," he said.
> "I know that," I said.
> "I thought you did," he said.
> "Sure," I said.
> "Let's go on back downstairs," he said. We went downstairs together.
> "Did you tell him?" my mother asked.
> "Everything," Uncle Jack said.
> I could have fainted with relief.[1]

As we walked together that afternoon, there was little chance that Jamie was aware of how his story would differ from many others, but I was about to tell him mine.

"One afternoon when I was fourteen my father gathered my brother and me together in the living room. Your grandma was away, and so we had the house to ourselves. Your grandpa, my dad, took out his medical books and explained sexuality and sexual morality to us. He was quite thorough and we talked for several hours. He particularly stressed the man's part in respecting and protecting the woman's well-being and reputation. He pointed out the damage done to women and children by not obeying God's laws on how we men were to behave with women."

This surprised Jamie. He was impressed and said so adding, "Grandpa told you to respect the women's part!" Although I tried to find out what Jamie meant, it was never clear to me exactly what surprised him. He was impressed though, and finally added, "I never thought of that before." New vistas were opening in his mind, and, from what could be seen, they appeared to be good ones. Who would know where this idea could lead?

Around us the view was opening up as we approached the cliff at the west end of the island. The trail branched with a short path reaching to the very edge of a three- to four-hundred-foot sheer drop to the ocean below. We got on our hands and knees to look over the edge, and it seemed that my stomach reached the bottom of the cliff in short order. Jamie must have felt something similar because we both backed away about the same time, having quickly filled our quota of excitement. There was, after all, nothing but rocks down there anyway, no reason to tarry.

Returning to the main trail, we resumed our topic. "One of the things that my dad told us that day were the family secrets. They are not things that the family likes to make a big deal about. Still we can learn a lot by remembering the past.

"Jamie, a little more than seventy years ago a naive country girl had to discover the secrets of life the hard way. Her parents never talked to her about sex. On the prairie where she grew up, young people went to church and other places together in horse-drawn buggies. One night when her boyfriend took her home from choir practice, he told her that he loved her very much and promised to marry her. She believed him completely and thought that he was telling her the truth. But he took advantage of her, and later he did not keep his promise. She was heartbroken when he left her. She was going to have a baby. She felt all alone and afraid.

"She prayed to her very best (and maybe only) friend something like this, 'Lord Jesus, you know that in my heart I was married to him. Please help me in my trouble.' Then when her baby girl was born, she prayed again, 'Lord, I give this child to you. Please take her and keep her for yourself.' She expected that God would take the baby to heaven right then! Instead the little girl grew healthy and strong.

"About three years later this lady met and married her true husband. He adopted the little girl and gave her his last name.

That baby was your grandmother."

I let the story's impact soak in before continuing. Jamie was thinking these things over, and it was obvious from the look on his face that the history lesson had not been lost on him. So instead of lecturing, I let him think. His face continued to be serious as he ducked, almost automatically, when a gull buzzed our heads. From here until we reached the top of the hill we would be fair game.

At length I interrupted his reverie. "There was quite a bit of suffering caused by your great-grandmother getting pregnant before she got married. Society has changed a lot, but there are still many problems to face when a girl gets pregnant at seventeen. These days there is birth control that can be used to help avoid getting pregnant and abortion to kill the child before it can be born. It is strange to think that if your great-grandmother had had an abortion, then your grandmother, you, and I would never have existed. Your great-grandmother was a woman of faith, even at seventeen. She gave her baby to God and expected that the baby would die and go to heaven. Instead she grew up and went as a missionary to South America for thirty years!"

We stopped a moment at the top of the hill to look out over the west end of the island and see the three other islands visible beyond it. It was strange how a few feet of elevation could make such a difference to both the view and the gulls who suddenly stopped their attacks. I mulled over how to talk about my parents' romance and life. Jamie knew most of the stories because at our request his grandpa had sat down with a tape recorder and told about his life. We had almost seven hours of what Jamie called one of his "favorite voices," telling stories of his life and times. These tapes were often requested at bedtime by both boys. Kitty had transcribed the stories that, with additions from other relatives, ran to one hundred forty pages. Jamie brought me back to the present.

"What's for snack?"

"Gorp," I said, bringing out some of the high-octane trail

mix with added M&Ms, raisins, and banana chips. All the dried fruit and nuts made us need our canteen as well. We stopped frequently because we could not walk and drink from a canteen without spilling it or smashing our lips.

Meanwhile, my mind returned to the problem of expressing the continuity of life. His grandparents' dating habits had produced a noticeable impact on his life even if he didn't know. My life had been guided and molded by the actions of my parents and grandparents without my knowing it either. My character bore the imprint of parents whose marriage began with a carefully nurtured relationship, a legacy I wished to pass on in my words and example to my sons. Finding the words was the problem at the moment.

I wanted my son to grasp the complexity and continuity of history. He needed to know that when he became a man his actions would matter very much. The life he received and the life he gave had long-reaching effects which could not be removed and which he should not ignore. Our sexuality is very much at the center of giving and receiving life, which is why the way a man lives with his sexuality matters so much. As I told him the history that had shaped him, Jamie began to pass into manhood by realizing that he would also write his page in the story.

What I ended up saying did not really satisfy. I went on about how times had changed since his grandparents had dated, but that they had taken the time to get to know each other through friends and school activities. That was an important part of their example to follow.

What I meant to say was, "How my parents and grandparents acted when they were dating had a big effect on me that I couldn't do anything about. I'm glad that they obeyed God's laws as much as they did because it has made my life, and now yours, a lot better than either of us realizes. You never know whose life you will be affecting when you start a relationship. That is something that boys don't think about when they are parked in a car with a girl."

We passed our camp just then and topped off our canteen from one of those water bottles that made our first day's hike so taxing. It was starting to look like we would have twice as much water as we needed.

"Let's give the extra water to someone, and then you won't have to carry it back," Jamie suggested.

"Splendid idea," I said, and with that we headed off on the short trail to the northern cliffs.

7

COLLISIONS
(Anacapa—Day 2)

———◆◆———

WE ARRIVED AT CATHEDRAL COVE. Here the trail ended at a rapidly sloping cliff edge. Unlike the cliff at the west end, which had so recently thrilled us, this area allowed the weary traveler several rocky ledges on which to sit before plunging down to the ocean below us. It was here, not three feet from a trio of fledgling gulls, that we settled in for the longest uninterrupted talk of the trip. For that reason I always remember this spot when recalling the talks we had. The sun was warm and the breeze cool. The view was magnificent, and the rocks were comfortable—as rocks go.

"What have you got left on your list?" I asked, feeling quite curious as to what his list might contain. Jamie produced a paper from his pocket and unfolded it four times. The left hand margin showed evidence of being torn out of a spiral note-book. He carefully folded the sheet and returned it to his pocket before he spoke.

"How old do you have to be to date?" he asked after finding the cozy corner of his rock.

"Well, I was not allowed any form of dating until I was fifteen." Not that this was the definitive word, but it provided a basis for comparison. "Actually, there are different kinds of dating that are good for different ages." This was news to Jamie and he looked up surprised but silent.

"The best way to start dating is through group dating. This is when a group of boys and girls go places and do things together. There are lots of chances to talk, play, or work together and get to know each other without the pressure of having to keep up a conversation or activity by yourself. You are starting to do things as part of the youth group at church already, but you just haven't thought of it as dating. At your age the activities are all planned for you. When you get to be fourteen or fifteen, you can choose a lot of the activities that you go to and probably the group you will go with as well.

"Part of the reason for choosing some of the groups you join is trying to get to know different people, especially girls, that interest you. Some people go to a lot of trouble to get in a group with someone they like. I don't think your reasons for joining have to be a secret. Some people might be embarrassed or afraid to be direct because they think they might not be liked in return. They won't talk about it, but you could just say, 'I'd like to be in this group to get to know you better.' That would be fine."

"I mean real dating, when you take the girl somewhere," Jamie interrupted. What I was talking about was too normal, too ordinary; he wanted something special. This was something that I wanted to avoid. There are too many pressures when kids think of dating as something different from their lives growing up. Dating should be a natural outgrowth of an expanding range of relationships. These words were not the ones for an eleven-year-old boy, however, so I tried again.

"Dating means enjoying something in the company of a girl, having fun while you go someplace together. If you enjoy yourself and include a girl, then you have a date. Dating is supposed to be fun.

"Sometimes it works the other way; you enjoy a girl's company and so you think of fun things to do together like you would with any of your friends. You can do that alone or in groups. Fun is fun."

"But isn't there something... you know, that makes it a date?"

"Well, Jamie, most people would call something a date if you made a direct invitation to a girl to do something with you. Like if you called her up and asked her to go with you on Friday night to a party."

"So how old do you have to be to do that?"

"Old enough to have an idea what you like to do and who you like to do it with. Even so, it is often better to start out with double dating—when two boys and two girls go somewhere together, then try solo dating after group dating. It all depends on how well you know the girl. When two people get together who don't know each other at all, it can get very tense, unless you are very comfortable with strangers.

"Solo dating has a lot to do with being old enough to drive alone because you have to get yourselves to your destination somehow. That usually means that double dating and solo dating start around age sixteen or seventeen."

"What do you do on a date?" Jamie asked. Although I had just covered this, now that I had answered his question, he was ready to listen to what I had to say.

"You have fun. You do the things that you would like to do, like going to ball games, concerts, parties, movies, or going out to eat; things like that. You do these things together with someone who might enjoy them too. Sometimes you might take walks or just sit and talk like we are doing now. Getting to know people can be fun. That is why group dating is a great way to start because you learn who likes the same things you do, and dating becomes inviting your friends to spend time with you—just like when you call them up to do things now."

"How do you pick a wife?" Jamie popped the big one.

"Do you think that is what dating is for?" I asked.

"Well, kinda…"

"I see."

"I want to find the right wife."

"That sounds like a good idea."

"So I was wondering how you find the best wife."

"You're too late because I married her, but let's see what we can do for you." I felt like a tailor fitting someone for a suit. Meanwhile we were both chuckling, the momentary tension relieved.

"There is no magic about it usually. You start out being friends. As you are getting to know women, you will find some that enjoy the things you do and some that enjoy you. When you find someone that enjoys you, and you find her very interesting, even fascinating, then you have a start. If you get to know her better and you want for each other the things that God wants, then think of marrying her.

"One other thing is prayer. I prayed about finding the right wife for a long time. Your grandmother tells me that she had prayed about it ever since I was born. So maybe praying is good for finding a good wife, and dating is good for making friends.

"Why don't I tell you how dating went for me."

"Good," said Jamie and he settled back into his rock and stopped playing with his shoes as he had during the last bit.

"As I said, my dad wouldn't let me date until I was fifteen. Dating at that time meant youth group activities or going to the park. There were usually about six to ten of us that walked together. We would talk, laugh, and have fun that way. We had girls that we liked especially well, and we would walk next to them lots of times.

"I used to help one of my girlfriends with her homework. Since my mom was her teacher, I found out that it upset my mom and to this day I don't know why. That is something that

I have noticed: what kids do on their dates often upsets their parents. This is a cause of lots of fights between parents and children in some families."

Jamie looked very sober but did not respond.

"I was just getting started with dating when something messed me up. As you know, your grandparents were missionaries, and they decided to send me to boarding school. What happened there kept me from dating for over two years. I reacted by treating girls, who I had previously regarded as friends, as alien and dangerous creatures. My friends and I would say of girls, 'They are despicable.' I wasn't sure what it meant, but it was not good, and girls were not good; so that was that."

"Why was it so bad, Dad?"

It wasn't so much the boarding school as something that happened there. It only took five minutes to impact my sexuality, self-esteem, and social poise for years. So I answered, "Here is what happened.

"I was summoned to the principal's office and I didn't know why. All the way there my mind whirled with what I might have done wrong. It couldn't be my schoolwork or my compliance with dormitory rules. My table manners were better than average, so what could it be?

"I recalled stories of students disappearing, never to return after holding hands with a girl or saying that they liked a certain girl. Still I had not broken the dreaded 'special friendship' rule.

"Had I inadvertently gotten closer than twelve inches to a girl? Well, I had sat next to one in the bus on the way to church. Sometimes there were an odd number of boys and girls and someone had to share a seat, but it was common knowledge that six inches and sometimes less were allowed when necessary on the bus.

"Then it came to me. It was Cindy! Cindy must have turned me in—but it had just been an accident. My mind whirled. Over Christmas break my brother and I were scheduled on the same flight as Cindy, so we were asked to escort her as far as Washington. On the plane she sat in the seat in front of mine. Perhaps it was her first flight, but she didn't know how to make the seat recline and asked me for help. While I was pointing out where the button was located, she moved her arm and my hand touched her forearm as I pulled back. My brother said it was an accident and that I wouldn't be in trouble, but here I was on my way to see 'The Doctor.'

"My anxiety was severe by the time I arrived at Doctor L's door. I had never been in this office before. The principal was sitting behind a big desk, and my counselor was standing to his left. One glance at their faces revealed that this was not a social visit. I sensed the beginning of the end of my schooling approaching rapidly. Still my mind was struggling to figure out what I had done wrong.

"'Please sit down.' I did. 'We called you here to ask you if you masturbated.'"

"I must have looked rather blank because one of them asked me if I knew what that meant. I said that I knew, and I didn't do that."

"What does *masturbation* mean?" Jamie interrupted. "I forgot."

"Oh! Masturbation is touching your genitals in a way that produces sexual pleasure. Both males and females can stimulate themselves this way. That is why I said 'genitals' instead of 'penis.'"

"I remember now," Jamie said, so I went back to the story.

"'Well,' the principal said, 'we wondered about whether you masturbated because you had such bad acne. If we can help you, please come and talk to us.'

"'I will,' I said and was dismissed. That was the second lie I told in those few minutes. The truth, Jamie, was that I did stimulate myself sometimes, but I was not going to tell them.

"I did not talk to anyone about my visit to the principal for at least a year until I got the nerve to tell my brother about my humiliation.

"Each new blemish on my face brought new shame as it was clear what people were thinking of me each time they looked at me. One day the school nurse told me (without my asking) that I had the worst case of acne in the school. I was afraid of what else she would say, but she didn't say anything. I really avoided girls then because how can you talk to a girl while she stands there looking at that zit thinking, 'I know what he does!'

"Now I knew that it wasn't true that self-stimulation caused acne, but what good did that do me if the rest of the world thought it did. You can't exactly walk up to people and casually ask, 'Say, are you one of those people who believes that masturbation causes acne?' The idea wasn't just for dummies either because Doctor L was a doctor of something and he believed it.

"Fortunately for me, my galloping hormones also started my facial hair growing. I was the only junior in high school with a beard. It got me a lot of teasing, but it was better than having the acne showing. I have had a beard ever since. Now I like to think that it is because I prefer to have a beard! Of course, the comment that my chin looks like Dudley Dooright of the Mounties, which your mom made when I did shave once, didn't help much either." (That cartoon was before Jamie's time and required some explaining.)

"In Bible school I was accused of being everything from a hippie to a drug dealer by fine Christian leaders because I had a beard and sort of long hair (over my shirt collar). They would quote the Scripture, 'a little leaven leavens the whole lump' to mean I was a bad influence on others. I was also not allowed to sing in the choir for the same reason, but none of that bothered me nearly like that visit to the principal's office."

"You must have felt bad," Jamie said after a bit. "You didn't say anything to anyone about it?" He looked mystified.

"That's right, Jamie. I was too embarrassed. I hope that if something strange like that happens to you, you will be able to talk to me, your mother, or someone about it. Having those secrets inside can hurt a lot." He nodded agreement.

"Why was your principal so upset?" Jamie wanted to know.

"About the masturbation, you mean?"

"Yeah! Why did you have to go to his office?"

"I don't know. Maybe he wanted to help me 'flee youthful lusts' or learn self-control. You see, some people can get quite out of control and masturbate to feel good the way others use drugs. If Doctor L wanted to help boys with those problems, he would have excellent motives, but the way he did things was all wrong. If he thought I had a problem, he chose a terrible way to show it. Neither he nor my counselor had ever had a conversation with me before, so I didn't trust them and calling me into the office only made it worse."

I took the binoculars and looked out over the cove for a while. There was more to the story than Jamie needed to hear right now. Sometime before he was an adult, we would no doubt talk about sexual functioning and problems. Then I would explain to him about sexual dysfunctions like the impotence and premature ejaculation that I developed from that visit to the office. For now we would dwell on normal development. Sometime though, I thought to myself, I will have to slip in the point that you can have sexual dysfunctions and correct them.

My experiences were not unique. Dean Kliewer in an excellent article entitled "Managing Sexual Feeling in the Christian Community" recounts his experience.

On another occasion, one of the part-time Immanuel teachers who saw himself as a counselor, took me aside and told me he knew I was taking sexual liberties with the girl I was dating. (That destroyed his credibility with me, because I was not into any kind of petting with the girl.)

His evaluation seemed related to my adolescent immaturity, my pimples, and to how I wore my corduroy trousers, way down on my hips, and tight at the ankles, in the absurd fashion of the time. He also told me that I was into self-stimulation. (He's got to be guessing again!)

I heard from him mainly that I was a rather wretched person. (True, but how could he have known that? I had never talked to him before.) Without the wisdom to share his evaluation with the principal, my parents, and a close family friend, this "counseling session" may well have greatly damaged my self-esteem.[1]

Doctor Kliewer had several advantages that I did not have. He was several years older than I was at the time and knew to talk to others about what had happened. In addition, his "counselor" destroyed his own credibility early in their visit, whereas I got the message right from the respected head of my school. A further factor for me was having my family and friends unavailable since I was away at boarding school. There was very little place to turn, so instead I spiraled down.

I did write some of my feelings in a letter to my old friend Jane.

About dating, you probably wouldn't want to date me if you saw me now. I am tall, six foot two inches to be exact, the tallest person here. I'm gangly, rather skinny, although I weigh 150 pounds which is very little for my size. I also have the worst case of acne in the school according to the nurse. That makes it rather bad because there are 29 or 30 guys here in school with acne. As a sideline I am an uncoordinated spaz.

The girls all have the idea that I am an antisocial brain. In a way I am because I don't go out of my way at all to be friendly to people who don't understand me. I don't make any effort to change their opinion of me. If you have any better ideas (like Ford does) tell me.

This probably sounds like a weird letter but I am feeling a little weird today. Just hope I am in a better mood next time you hear from me.

If you think my case was sad, think how very much worse it is for those who receive these sorts of messages about themselves from their own parents. Parents are very hard to displace as the final authority on a child's value or character—even if they are tragically wrong.

The whole experience at that school left me with something else to wrestle with as well. This was the result of several very conflicting messages that I was picking up. The reason my parents gave for sending me to this school was to learn proper Christian social skills. These were part of the stated objectives of the school itself. Therefore, we learned that while we could not stand together before a meal, we needed to sit boy-girl around the table and seat the girl to our left. Having a special friendship was reason for expulsion, but dating was mandatory for at least two functions a year.

The message seemed to be "do not like girls… but be sure to date them, do not be attracted to girls… but you will be punished for not interacting with them." Thus, several boys started a non-dating club to escape the tension and provide support to each other, but they were harassed and belittled by faculty and students and ordered by their counselors to take part in the mandatory dating socials or serve several weeks detention.

The message to not have a friendship with a girl or be attracted to her, but to date so that I wouldn't be bad or defective socially, shredded my insides. All I had known previously was that friendship with girls was primary and after that maybe you might date someone you liked. Here, you could not date the same girl twice in one month, so there was little danger that any friendship might develop. However, there was plenty of time for lust or fear to develop.

Here I was, trying to be a Christian and feeling all confused and tense. Then my mind started to play tricks on me. I began to find myself thinking sexually about the other boys. You could, after all, be friends and like them without having the ax fall on your neck. These feelings disturbed me immensely, but lasted for a long time. Even after I married, when a couple would walk into a room, I would look at the man first before looking at his female companion.

With the help of my wife who patiently, if uncomfortably, listened to my feelings, I was able to resolve this conflict by the fourth year of our marriage. It was most comforting to me that she, a fine Christian woman, thought that attraction between men and women was normal and even healthy. The final breakthrough came as she was able to discover that it is possible for men and women to be friends. With this discovery and acceptance, the cramp in my sexuality began to relax and the attraction to men disappeared. I count myself fortunate, but not unusual.

These thoughts circled my mind as Jamie and I looked about the kelp beds for marine life. This side of my history would remain unmentioned until such a time as he was facing these issues in his life. There was no need to talk about everything at this point. The whole idea was to help him know what to expect normally and prepare him for that. He also needed to know that not everything would develop normally at times. Eventually many problems can be corrected. I felt in no rush to talk about everything. Time was still on my side.

I returned to my story intent on facing the sexual attraction problem. This conflict was more difficult to talk about because it remains unresolved for me and, I suspect, most males.

"After attending boarding school for a year, I went to public high school. There they had very few rules and strange things like miniskirts. At boarding school the girls' dresses had to touch the bottom of their knees when sitting, so this was very different.

"I have found that one of the things that is hardest for me is to stop myself from peeking inside women's clothes when there is a chance.

"I remember in World History class there was one girl who would cheat all the time. During tests, she would lean across an aisle and copy from my paper. She wouldn't stop, and I was always afraid that I would get in trouble with the teacher. Finally I taught myself to write upside down and backwards so that she couldn't read my answers, but when I turned the paper back over it came out right.

"This girl wore the shortest dresses in the class. On the day of the first test when I wrote upside down and backwards she got angry at me because she couldn't read my answers. Soon after that she came into class wearing her miniskirt, sat down across from me and plopped her feet up on the corners of my desk. I would not look over at her, although part of me wanted to a lot. She sat there laughing at me, while I got very tense. The side of my nose that faced her started to twitch."

"Why did your nose twitch?" Jamie wanted to know.

"I guess that I was more nervous than I knew how to handle, so my muscles started to jump. I have gotten that twitch back every spring since then. I also get that twitch whenever I feel very tense.

"Sometimes now I meet ladies with very short dresses or loose blouses, and I know I could look inside their clothes. I try to look at their eyes, but sometimes I get too curious and peek. Then I feel some relief of the curiosity, but I'm also angry because I feel like I lost. Job said in the Bible that he had made a covenant with his eyes not to look upon a woman. Sometimes the part of me that wants to look is still stronger than the part of me that doesn't.

"When I was in about first grade, my parents went out for an evening and left me with a babysitter. She was probably about eighteen years old. She was wearing one of those dresses that was fluffed up and it bounced while she walked. Sometime that evening, I went over and tried to see what was under that bouncy thing. I must have thought it was a bad thing to do because I would never have tried it with my parents around. When I tried to lift her dress, she laughed and swatted it back down.

"She shook her finger at me laughing and said, 'Now stop that, you naughty boy.' I kept trying to look under her dress until she finally got cross. It seemed like an exciting game and I guess I thought she liked it too—for a while.

"When my folks got home she must have told them, because any doubts I might have had about whether it was wrong to look under ladies' dresses were quickly dispelled. I went to bed with my rear end reminding me not to do that again! While that settled the question of what was the right thing to do, my curiosity was not so easily taught."

Jamie had never acted overtly curious, but I thought I'd ask anyway. "Jamie, are you ever curious about what people look like under their clothes?"

"Sometimes," he said. "It is sort of a curiosity that comes every once in a while. I wonder if I am maturing late or something to that effect."

"There can be a lot of pressure to want to be normal. Isn't it funny that when people say 'normal' they usually mean 'being the same as everyone else'? Actually, 'normal' is being a little bit different from everyone else. Still there is that curiosity in us all about how we are the same or different from others. We want to look and find out.

"There are social rules that say that a boy or man cannot look directly at another's genitals. If you do, you are likely to be called names or punched in the nose. The only exceptions are the strong, dominant, aggressive males that will look at others, point, and make fun of weaker boys. Those dominant boys have strong bodies or are part of strong groups, but their spirits and character are weak. Otherwise, they wouldn't have to stoop so low and make fun of others.

"One of the things that many boys hate about junior high is taking showers in gym. Mean things get said and done there, like snapping kids' private parts with towels or making fun of those who develop later than others."

"Why do kids do that in junior high?" he asked. "It gives me a strange feeling, sort of a tingling down my spine."

"Yes. It is kind of scary to think of someone snapping you or even watching it happen to someone else. It makes us feel sort of powerless."

Jamie nodded. "Is there anything you can do?"

"Not a lot. You can stand up for weak guys, but if they pick on you then it is best to have friends near you. You can also walk away or try resisting.

"Here is some psychological advice. If you resist, then match the force the attacker is using. If you use less, they don't stop. If you use more, they try to stop you. If that happens, then it just gets worse. It doesn't seem that anything works very well.

"Making people feel powerless is part of the reason for being mean. If you are mean and tough, you can feel powerful. Kids like that! Especially kids who have felt powerless a lot—like those from unloving families.

"In junior high, kids try out their power on each other. By that age they know how to organize and plan so they can form powerful groups that they couldn't when they were younger.

"Kids in junior high still don't feel powerful enough to challenge adults most of the time, but by the time that they reach high school many teens are ready to try their power on adults—usually teachers and parents. This often makes for some mighty fights because adults don't like to have their power challenged. Adults don't like to feel powerless or controlled any more than kids do. That is why adults are often mean."

Maybe it was talking about big scary things or just the sound of the surf that made Jamie pick up the binoculars and look across the horizon. We kept hoping for a glimpse of the orca that had been reported near here.

"All I see is California," he said before dropping his view to the kelp bed that also produced nothing. It seemed all the action was right where we were.

8

DANGEROUS CURVES
(Anacapa—Day 2)

———◆◆◆———

DO YOU KNOW THAT BRASH LITTLE GULLS, who couldn't even fly, kept running right past us? Jamie wanted to feed them but we had no food. He tossed little pebbles their way instead if they got too close. For some reason there were no adult gulls buzzing us here. Perhaps this was established human territory, and even their parents viewed the adolescent birds as interlopers.

"Tell me about how you started dating," Jamie said. Dating was the "real thing" in his mind and he wanted to know how it worked.

"Very well. You remember that I quit having anything to do with girls after that boarding school. It got a little bit better during my last year of public high school. About this time your mother and I met for the first time, and we couldn't stand each other. Soon after that my family spent a summer in our old town with my good friends from before boarding school. It was especially good to spend a summer with these old friends since the boys saw nothing wrong with liking girls or the girls with liking boys. They still liked me! When I got older, I found out that my father had worked very hard to arrange that summer trip for us and I appreciate that very much.

"By the time that I was back to relating with women, I was in Bible school, and it was a bumpy start. The pace was much too fast. The first step was often a date with someone I didn't know at all. I preferred going canoeing on a date since there was a great deal to observe around us on a lake, and the social demands were few. No one asked, 'What is the proper decorum for a canoe?' Decorum is the right way to behave," I said in response to a questioning look before continuing.

"I invited one girl canoeing several times but she always sent someone else in her place. It did not take long to become tired of that! I diverted my energy instead to the study of body language and people's nonverbal cues and reactions.

"This phase is always somewhat embarrassing to remember although your mother, who I met again at that time, loves to tell stories. But, I am getting ahead of myself.

"I was eighteen at this time. The hypocrisy in religion got to be too much for me. I was not sure what I believed, so I quit doing what I had always done and started over with only what I could find for myself in the Bible as a guide. One result of this was to struggle with my fractured sexual self. It was important for me to restore my relationships with the female half of the human race.

"You see, one of the things that showed up when I read about Jesus was that he had women around him and got along very well. I began to pray that I would be able to see and relate with women in the same way as Christ related with women. He related with women frequently, comfortably, and without being sexual with them. This fit with much of my father's words and example, although I did not realize it at the time.

"Things didn't always go smoothly. I dated one girl who reached down one night and began to rub my penis through my pants.

"Touching each other's genitals is called 'heavy petting.' It felt good, but at the same time I felt rather frightened, out of control and in danger. When I asked her to stop, she seemed surprised and said that she thought that was what all men wanted. I asked her if it wouldn't make her uncomfortable if I were to touch her genitals and she said, 'Yes.' Here we had the basis for some understanding and communication. In time we became friends.

"You know, Jamie, that story does not seem quite fair to the girl because of something that had happened a few weeks earlier with the same girl. One time when I kissed her, I rubbed her breasts. Since she didn't seem to mind, I did it some more and even put my hand inside her blouse. This is called 'light petting.' It seemed exciting at the time, although I sure hoped that no one would find out. I probably gave her the idea that I was one of those boys who like to 'pet,' so I had it coming!

"Do you suppose that she might have felt just as mixed up and scared when I was touching her as I did when she was touching me, but she could not speak up?"

Jamie nodded, "I think she would have."

"Many boys will tell you that this is exciting stuff, but I feel mostly sad when I remember those two nights. I talked to God about it and asked him to forgive me and help me be more loving. You know what? He did!

"On my first date with another girl, she snuggled up to me and put her face up to be kissed, so I did. Her lips were slippery and what she did with her tongue reminded me of what snails do with their tongues on the glass sides of aquariums. It was revolting. It wasn't at all like what Jane had described or anything that I have felt since. Not everything is as good as the advertising. When I got to know your mom, she was a very nice kisser. But I'm getting ahead of myself again.

"One summer, while I was working as a camp counselor for inner-city children and their mothers, I made a lot of friends. One of them was a girl named Linda. One day during a severe thunderstorm I came across Linda huddled in a corner sobbing. She managed to say that she was afraid of the lightning, so I put my hands on her head and prayed for her that the fear would be healed; then I began to sing a happy praise hymn. Before the end of the first verse, she was singing along. We sat together through the rest of the storm and watched the fascinating light show outside. During the rest of that summer, she was not frightened by lightning again, although she told me that she had felt afraid all her life. This event was one of those that led me toward psychology."

"That is very interesting," Jamie said. "I always wonder about the things that got you started in psychology." Then he added, "It seems very unusual for someone around the age of twenty to still be afraid of lightning." I nodded.

"One night during the summer a group of us went down to the beach to pray. By morning the only two left were Linda and I. There was a story going around in those days that an evangelist named Arthur Blessit had seen Jesus walking on the water, so toward morning I was praying for a chance to see Jesus walk on the water as well. After a long time had passed, I was on my knees praying earnestly to see Jesus when I felt a strong urging to look up. When I looked out towards the water in the first light of dawn, I was very disappointed that all I saw was Linda walking down the beach.

"I sat there dejected for I was certain that I was going to see something, when a quiet voice inside me said, 'The only place you will see me is inside others.' I was quiet a long time. From then on I began to look for Christ's presence in others, and you know, that helped me see women more like Jesus saw them."

"How long did it take you to see women the way Christ saw them?" Jamie wanted to know.

I laughed at the very thought. "Oh wow, Jamie! I'm still working on that one and probably will always be. It did not take long to start seeing results though. That was encouraging.

"Linda and I began to talk about sexuality one day when I noticed she was upset, and she told me she had severe menstrual cramps."

"What are menstrual cramps, Dad?"

"Well, Jamie, menstrual cramps are a kind of pain that some women have during menstruation. Sometimes it is so bad that they have to take medicine and go to bed for a day or two. Other women don't have any discomfort at all. I suppose it feels a little like the cramp you feel if you really have to have a bowel movement—except that it might last a day or two.

"Anyway, I prayed for her cramps, and a few days later she thanked me and said something about it being strange to tell a boy about her cramps. She said that she had never talked about sexual things very much, and I agreed that I usually avoided it too.

"One night a few weeks later, when all the little camping monsters had gone home, we took a walk to the cliff where that week we had taught the campers to climb. We sent them up and down as many times as they would go to be sure that they would be tired enough to sleep some that night. On our walk Linda told me about herself. As we sat on the top of the cliff and watched the moon and stars, she cried a lot about the way boys had treated her. She asked me many questions about sex and boys, most of which I could answer."

"Did sitting and talking with Linda encourage your career in psychology?" Jamie wanted to know. I thought to myself, this guy is a regular little interviewer. This feels like being on a talk show, but my answer was more to the point.

"It might have contributed indirectly. It did remind me of the times that Jane would explain about boys and girls. This time it was my turn to explain.

"Actually, Jane had never talked directly to me about sex the way that Linda and I did that night. Sometimes while we were talking I would think how strange it was to be sitting out on a hill alone at night explaining to a girl about sex. Because I felt close to her, I would feel like touching her, but I remembered that Jesus was to be seen inside her, and I tried to explain things just like I would to Jesus. I have a good feeling about our talk, but it also seems like a very risky thing to do. I wouldn't try it the same way again because as I have gotten older I have become less trusting."

"What do you mean by trusting?" Jamie inquired. He didn't seem uncomfortable with his question, just lost. I'll admit I wasn't sure myself what all I meant.

"That is a good question. Let's see if I can answer it." I paused for a while. Jamie says that sometimes when he asks me a question it takes so long for me to answer that he has forgotten what he asked. This time he chased a couple of adolescent gulls while I thought.

"I think it works like this, Jamie. My dad taught me to protect women, but I didn't learn until much later about protecting myself. I had a pretty good idea how I planned to behave, but I really didn't know Linda that well. It turned out that she was also a loving person, so I was safe. God must have looked out for me. You see, the best way to be safe is to stay out of dangerous situations altogether—if you can. If I had known this at the time, I would never have gotten in the next situation that came along that summer."

⸺⸺•◦•⸺⸺

"You see, sexual temptation did show up that summer when I was put in charge of a cabin full of women. The camp, which was run by a major denomination to meet the needs of the Chicago inner-city, was short one female counselor, so I was appointed to a cabin full of young mothers. The cabin was equipped with a private room for the counselor, so I agreed. If I had thought about protecting myself, I would not have taken the job.

"Being in charge of the women's cabin somehow also gave me the job of coordinating all the activities for every woman in camp. As I took them on walks, I would listen to them talk about me in a foreign language. They did not know that I understood what they were saying. What they had to say was quite graphically sexual, with some nice comments about my legs thrown in. Finally, several of the women from my cabin came to me and asked if I wanted to make love to them. They said that their husbands were no doubt at home enjoying themselves with other women and they didn't want to miss out. When I declined the offer, they pointed out that they were married women, so I didn't have to worry about pregnancies or diseases. I don't remember what I told them, but by the end of the week they were behaving themselves except for the remarks about my legs."

"What diseases were those ladies talking about, Dad?"

"They are called venereal diseases, or VD for short. They are diseases that you can only get from having sex with an infected partner."

"How do you know if you have venereal diseases or not?" Jamie wanted to know.

"The best way to know that you do not have venereal diseases is having only one sexual partner who also has only had one sexual partner—you.

"When Rami was born, we did not have drops put in his eyes for gonorrhea because your mother and I knew that we had only been with each other. Gonorrhea is one kind of VD.

"You can't get most forms of VD if you only have one faithful partner. This is not always possible because of rape and incest. There are medical tests and lists of symptoms for different diseases." We then discussed the more common ones like gonorrhea, syphilis, herpes, trichomoniasis, and gardnerella.

I can't believe that I forgot to talk about AIDS, but AIDS was not around when I was growing up. This form of VD can be passed on through blood and intravenous drug use as well as sex. When we got home, we took time to discuss AIDS as well. Fortunately, through television and school, Jamie already had a lot of information about the disease. Our family is keeping up-to-date as new information comes out. At the same conference where I first learned about AIDS, then called *Karposi's Sarcoma*, we learned about another health threat, cervical cancer. This I did remember to mention.

"Having many sexual partners before age nineteen may lead to cancer of the cervix in women." Getting out the diagrams, I pointed out the cervix. "This spot is covered with very few cells when women are sixteen. That makes it easy for the sperm to penetrate living cells with foreign protein. Foreign proteins like DNA are not good for living cells. Of course, getting into other cells is what sperm do best since that is their job when they get to the ovum. In the cervix, though, they are up to no good. The more sexual partners a girl has had the more types of foreign protein can get in.

"By the time a girl is nineteen, her cervix is covered by a layer of dead cells that is hundreds of cells thick. That is rather good insulation. There is reason to suspect that this may protect her from cervical cancer when she gets older. These are things that kids do not think about when they start having sex."

"But, I have gotten away from my story. Your mother and I got acquainted because she was the person who answered the phones on weekends at the school we were both attending. I liked to try little body language 'experiments' on her, like changing the direction in which my legs were crossed when sitting next to her to see how she changed her posture, or how long it took her to recross her legs, and she liked the attention. Since she was always around, we could get to know each other. We did things with groups and were friends before I asked her on our first official date. I think that is the way dating is supposed to progress.

"It was hard to get her to talk at first because I don't think that she had ever been friends with a boy. She had lots of boyfriends but not a boy friend," I said, pausing a long time between *boy* and *friend* to make the point. "Our first official date was on Valentine's Day. Four months later we were engaged.

"One of the things that I liked about your mother was that

she was interested in a sexual relationship. She thought that it would be fun when we were married. Knowing that helped me feel more accepted and relaxed with her. I was not really sure until then if sexual feelings were something that only men had. It was good to find out that women have sexual feelings too. It was scary but what a nice discovery. It seemed natural to her, so I don't think she ever knew how much that helped me. I feel all warm inside right now, even as I think about her.

"Somewhere around the time that your mother and I got engaged we had a discussion about the phrase, 'If you love me, you will have sex with me.' I had always hated the phrase as did she. I told her that I loved her and that if I ever tried to have sex with her before we were married that she could know for a solid fact—regardless of what I said—I did not love her. I didn't try to see how close I could get physically either. We kissed and hugged and that is where it stopped.

"You know, Son, a lot of people will think that I am pretty weird for that, but it is something that I have never been sorry about. In my work I talk to a lot of women and have to keep a lot of secrets, but your mom knows by her experience that she can trust me, and I know that I can trust her. This has given me years of peace of mind. Besides that, we can enjoy sex, which is part of the whole idea, without having any guilt feelings about each other.

"After your mother and I got engaged, some well-meaning, concerned relatives came to warn us that now we were engaged, it would be hard to keep from having sex with each other. This hurt my feelings because of the promise that I had made to your mother. I felt misunderstood. We were young and many people seemed to have doubts about our motives and behavior.

"They were right about one thing though—we have to take our sexuality very seriously because it can be a powerful force. That is part of why I didn't take chances with seeing how sexual I could be and still stop myself. Stopping those kinds of feelings is not easy and goes against our nature.

"Attraction and sexual feelings are easy to come by, but getting to know someone is harder. It takes a long time. Getting acquainted can get completely lost in sexual feelings. Petting is exciting, and many kids can get into sex instead of getting to know each other. People can get high on sex just like they do with drugs.

"I know that sexual attraction is strong. Even now—at my advanced age—it is too hard for me to be in control in every situation, so the only alternative is not to get in some situations. For example, when we go camping with other couples and I will be there alone with some other lady, I always arrange to have children along with us. Things are much more relaxed that way, and we can enjoy each other's company."

This evoked some thoughts about friendship. "During the engagement and after we got married, I found out that I had to give up my friendships with women. This was necessary in order to devote the time your mother and I needed to get adjusted to each other. This provided security for your mom, who did not understand those kinds of friendships at the time. She grew up with a brother but without having a chance to have friendships with boys—so that did not make any sense to her.

"I also had less time for my friendships with guys. Marriage takes a lot of work and time to get going. Soon we started to have more mutual friends. I still saw my old male friends; we had a band, and we still played together and got a few 'gigs.'

"After the first year, there was more time for friends. Eventually most of our friendships with others were doing well, although it took some years and therapy for your mother to discover friendships with the opposite sex. She can tell you how hard it is to not learn about them when you are growing up." Then I told Jamie about various people he knew as his parents' friends and how they had come to be friends to one or both of us.

"You know, I have found that we expect people that we don't know to be like people we do know.

"I remember when I was living in South America, a photographer from the United States came to visit. He was a black man. Every time I would see him I would start to talk to him in Spanish without thinking. I expected him to be like all the other black people I knew who spoke Spanish. He would give me this funny smile and say, 'I'm sorry, little boy, I don't speak Spanish.' I would always be surprised, and then embarrassed. When I came to the United States, I did the same thing. I spoke to all black people in Spanish; it is what I expected them to understand."

Jamie shot me a look of disbelief and maybe disdain. "That's dumb!" he pronounced.

"You could be right there! Still, it was what I expected, and what we expect has a big effect on what we see and do.

"There are girls and women who have been raised a lot differently from you or me. They do things that we might not expect. I expected that all women would act like my mother or your mother, so I got some surprises!

"When I was working as an electronic repairman, one of the ladies from church asked me to look at her stereo. We set up an appointment for the next day at four in the afternoon. When I rang the doorbell the next afternoon at the arranged time, she came to the door in a bathrobe with her hair in a towel. She said she had forgotten I was coming over, but to come in and she would show me the stereo. I followed her to the stereo feeling somewhat uncomfortable. The room with the stereo turned out to be her bedroom, and instead of leaving me with the malfunctioning device, she sat on the bed.

"I quickly devoted myself to the examination of the machine and within a minute found it was a *mess* (a technical term). When I turned to tell her that it needed to go into the shop for repairs, she was sitting in such a way as to show me that she had nothing on under her bathrobe. I felt tense, afraid, and a little dizzy, so I quickly began to gather my test equipment while she told me that she did not want to spend the money to send the stereo to the shop. I said, 'That's fine, call me if you want it fixed,' and headed for the door.

"When I got home, I told your mother all about what happened. She said, 'We will have to be careful with Mrs. Smith,' and I agreed. Mrs. Smith never treated me any differently after that—which surprised me a little. As far as I know, the stereo still doesn't work."

Jamie looked off towards the kelp bed below for a while. "I think it would be strange to have someone from church do that," he said finally. "I always think that church people will be good."

"Sometimes, I wonder if there are any differences between church people and other people. When it comes to sexual trouble, most studies seem to find as many problems with each group."

"That doesn't sound too good," Jamie said with a wry smile.

"It is tough!" I agreed. "That's part of why I said earlier that I'm not as trusting anymore. You will have to set the standards for yourself and not expect that even Christians will help you keep them. I hope you accept God's standards for yourself."

Jamie nodded enthusiastically, and it warmed me inside. Looking around our temporary home on the island, it seemed wonderful to want God's standards. Would it seem the same to Jamie five years from now on a date or with a class full of peers who saw things differently? The need to actively select and maintain one's own standards led me to think of added problems.

"Many people, both men and women, have been rejected and will be very afraid of rejection. They will either stay away or be very dependent on you. Some of them will try to do almost anything they think will keep you from rejecting them.

"Women who have been sexually abused or who come from families who don't know how to be affectionate often confuse sex with affection. Did you know that one out of four women has been sexually attacked at some time? Someone even tried to attack your mother; it affected her for years." I told him the story.

"Some of the girls you date or know will have been sexually abused. Some may not even remember that it happened. Many of these girls think that all men want is sex. They do not know what it is like to have a boy as a friend. You will need to teach them about being friends. Abused girls often try to have sex with you so that you won't leave them or attack them. They think giving you sex will make you be nice to them and want them. It is very sad."

Jamie nodded, "I feel sorry for those people." His voice was a little choked up. He started to say something else but stopped. Then his mind turned to the challenge before him. "Being a man is harder than I thought." His face took on a determined look. I decided to test him a bit.

"Many boys cannot tell the difference between sex and affection either. They want to feel accepted and special so they try to have sex as much as possible. We all need affection, but no one absolutely needs sex. What is the difference between affection and being sexual, Jamie?"

With a quick smile he replied, "Affection is just liking someone and being a friend with them. Being sexual means that you want to have sex with them or pet them, something like that."

Those were the basics, and I told him so, but pressed for more. "What kind of touching goes with being affectionate?"

"Touching of their private spots."

"Wrong!" I said, knowing that he hadn't listened to the question. "I said, 'being affectionate.'"

"Oh, being affectionate! Oh! I see! Umm..." He recovered and thought for quite a while. Finally, he laughed nervously and said, "I'm not quite sure, Dad."

"Well, how about the ways we kiss or hug with our family or friends?"

"Yes, a friendly kiss or hug," he said laughing. "Thanks for helping me!"

"As long as you keep asking yourself whether you are touching to show affection or to be sexual, you will do all right. That is important even after you are married, so that both your wife and your kids will know the difference.

"It is also important to ask permission before hugging someone when you don't know if they want to be hugged or if they don't know what your hug means. Hugs can mean different things. Be sure to talk about the meaning of what you do. This is when being sensitive and a good listener pays off for you. It is the best way to find out what is going on inside someone else. I know that you are a sensitive person, so you have a good start."

"Can you be too sensitive?" Jamie asked. "Sometimes I think that I'm too sensitive."

"What do you mean?"

"Well, I feel hurt or sad if something bad happens to someone," he said, checking out his shoes. "When I hear about sad things, I feel like crying." He continued to look away.

I was filled with a warm feeling for this boy, so I reached out, put my arm around him, and gave him a squeeze. He snuggled up, and I sort of rocked him while answering.

"I think it is terrific that you are sensitive. I don't think that there is any such thing as being too sensitive. It is just that the world can be very hurtful for sensitive people, and you need to learn ways to protect yourself from being hurt.

"It is like those cactus we saw. They are very soft and full of water on the inside, but on the outside God has given them tough skin and needles to protect their soft parts from being dried out or eaten. You need to protect yourself from dangerous people, so you won't be eaten. You need to keep away from hurtful people, so you won't dry out. Then you can be sensitive to those whom you trust."

"How can I tell which are the dangerous people?" he asked staying close.

"Now there you have it made!" I said. "Since you are a sensitive person, you need only listen to the warnings of your heart. When a voice inside says, 'Look out' or, 'Something is not right here,' then avoid that place or person unless you have a clear command from God to do something different."

We were quiet for a while. That usually meant that some thoughts were milling around waiting to find enough order or strength to come charging out. While we sat I took off my cap, grateful that my "beak" was not needed for protection here. The breeze blew unobstructed across the top of my head as I gathered my thoughts.

9

AN UPHILL CLIMB
(Anacapa—Day 2)

———◆◆◆———

A S WE SAT THERE ON THE EDGE of the cliff and watched
the brown pelicans fly in formation, I checked my list of
topics and found one of the tougher ones that I had left for the
end. It seemed better to have covered some basics first.

"Jamie," I said, putting away the list, "as you were growing
up you were exposed to several sexual situations that you may
or may not remember. Sometimes these memories come back
to people later, causing trouble or puzzling them, so I figured
that we should talk about them a little." We watched a couple
of sea lions chase through the kelp beds below us.

"When you were four years old, we had a lot of video tape
equipment in our apartment because of research projects I was
involved in. This was in the days when only professionals had
video recorders. In fact, the one-half inch cassettes were very
new.

"One afternoon one of the men I was working with at the
time came over to get something. When I came back in the
room with whatever it was he wanted, I found him using the

machine to watch a tape of a lady having oral sex with a man. You were standing right beside him watching. I was pretty mad and switched the machine right off. I can't remember what I said to him, but he thought it was all rather funny. I told him to leave, so he did. Do you know what 'oral sex' is?"

He shook his head no. We were both rather uncomfortable with this topic. I remembered how the Song of Songs said three times, "Do not arouse desire before its time," and discussing the ethics, techniques, and details of sexual pleasuring seemed better left until he was preparing for a marriage relationship. General knowledge about the subject, it seems, is needed much earlier these days. I would have been happy to say that people use almost every part of their bodies to rub each other and leave it at that for now. But if I disliked explaining fellatio to an eleven-year-old, it was worse when he was four.

"You didn't know what it was then either. You asked me, 'Daddy, what was that lady doing with that man's penis?' So I asked you what you saw, and you told me that the lady had the man's penis in her mouth. So I explained that the lady was kissing the man's penis and holding it in her mouth which some ladies did when they were older and married. You made a face, and I said people did a lot of other strange things that someday you would learn about. You said you didn't like those things, which I replied was fine. I was sorry that you had seen any of this at all.

"You asked me about it again a few days later, so we reviewed it. You also did a lot of pointing to your brother's penis and laughing after baths for a few days. Do you remember any of this?"

Jamie laughed nervously and shook his head no. It was not particularly good news to me that he did not remember. No conscious memory does not mean that there were no effects from his exposure to pornography. That is why we talked about it. If he knew consciously what happened to him, he would be able to make sense of any peculiar reactions he might have later in life.

Since we can't prevent all bad things from happening to our children, it is important to talk about each event and the feelings that went with it. Jamie and I had just talked about one incident, but the next one was harder. What made it tough was my feeling that better planning, on my part, could have prevented the problem. Still, Jamie needed to know about and discuss his experiences.

"You also opened the bedroom door and walked in on your mother and me when we were making love three different times. Remember when you were little, how we kept trying to teach you to knock before you opened the door?" He laughed but kept watching the sea lions. "We finally got a lock for the door, which you might want to remember if you ever have children like you!" A small smile greeted this remark. "It was dark whenever you came in, but I wondered if you saw or heard anything that made you curious!"

Jamie thought for a while, then said he could not remember anything unusual. He remembered middle-of-the-night trips after scary dreams and so we talked about some of those.

"It was nice to have someone to talk to when I had a scary dream. You listened to me better, 'cause Mom kept falling asleep, but I really liked it when she prayed for me that Jesus would stay with me all night."

Just then the two lady campers sat down near us and struck up a conversation about the best place to watch the sunset. It was unusual to have them talking to us. Things seemed to change when you were out away from civilization.

When these same two ladies had arrived at camp a day and a half ago, they had been very different. They would talk to the couples in camp but reserved those stony glares for Jamie and me that women customarily give to predatory males as if to say, "We do not wish to be disturbed!"

It is interesting to note the different strategies that people develop to avoid attack and predation. While snorkeling around the bay the next day, Jamie and I were able to watch many fish at close range that would have sped out of sight when we approached them on a mainland beach. Here in a marine preserve they seemed to lack the fear of man that their mainland kin possessed. One can see the signs of humanity's predatory behavior in the way others respond.

It was either the effect of the island or the way we kept to ourselves that now encouraged these two ladies to smile and talk. Since we had come to this rock in the Pacific to be alone, we bid them "good afternoon" after five minutes or so and went for a walk to increase our appetites for that camp food supper.

"Do you have another topic on your list?"

"We have covered a lot of them already," he said as he studied the unfolded page. "What about rock and roll?"

"What about it?" I asked, being caught a little off guard by the question. At the same time I was glad that he had not left the list-making to me, because there were several important parts of adolescence which he included that I had completely overlooked. I was impressed.

"Well," Jamie said, "I hear a lot about rock and roll at church, and I wondered if it was good or bad. I know you listen to some, so I wanted to know."

"I'm glad you brought that up. I had forgotten all about that business, and it is something that parents and their children often fight about." Jamie looked pleased.

"I guess rock music is like fruit; it comes in good, bad, or, in most cases, a mixture of both. In the market we won't buy fruit if it is rotten, but sometimes if it has just a little bad spot we will. Then we eat the good and throw out the bad.

"Now some people say that they only listen to the music, but I usually sing to myself most of the time when I am alone. I try to listen to music with words I like to hear over and over. That is how we choose the music that you boys listen to when you are falling asleep at night. Of course, a lot of it is classical music with no words.

"One of the reasons that I like to record my albums on tapes is that I can leave off songs that I don't like."

Jamie remembered being there and hearing me eliminate songs with objectionable lyrics from my tapes. We talked about songs that were omitted from my collection even though they had very appealing music. I also pointed out that much of my rock music was by Christian artists. Being selective isn't just for rock music, so I tried to make another point.

"Just as bad as rock and roll is the country-and-western music that your mother likes." Jamie smiled, thinking of my euphemisms for country music. "There aren't satanic country albums like there are rock albums, but most of what they say about men and women, sex, and alcohol is a long way from Christian values. For that matter, there is even some Christian music that says things that I won't play. I don't agree with everything that I listen to, but I eliminate the things that hurt me or that I think will hurt you. In fact, a good standard is to ask if the music will make us stronger, healthier, or holier.

"When it comes to music or other things where we must choose what is good for us, people often quote a verse in the Bible that tells us not to do anything that will make another Christian stumble. Most people who quote that mean to say, 'Don't do things that I don't like or that upset me.' People are entitled to be upset all they want over matters of personal taste. Everyone has the right to dislike or be angry about anything they wish. It is not too good for them, and it is certainly unpleasant to be around, but it is their privilege. Look at it this way, if it seems that a weak Christian might sin because of what I choose, then I will change. If it seems that strong Christians won't like it, I recognize that they are entitled to their opinions, but I may not change."

We stopped to look at gum plants again. What happened to all that sap as the flower bloomed? What use did that milky gum on the blossoms serve? We didn't know. Sometimes things have uses that we never imagine. For instance, pubic hair serves as a natural lubricant so people don't rub off all their skin. Who thought up that plan? The sap on the plants, however, would remain a mystery. As we walked, Jamie pulled out his list. He was ready for the next topic.

"What should be your life's ambition?"

"To be everything God created you to be: Special, unique, and just as important as everyone else—no matter what you do." I thought that was pretty eloquent. Jamie was not impressed.

"I mean like a job."

"A job should provide your needs and give you something to share with others. Better yet, you should like what you do. Remember this, though, nothing you do is all that important. Who you are comes first. There is nothing you can do or achieve that God won't consider destroying to make you the kind of person he intended you to become."

After walking in silence for a while, I broke the reverie. "What about your idea of becoming an actor or an architect?" I smiled to myself, wondering if he took his career preferences in alphabetical order.

"Yeah!" he said, and we shared the excitement of dreams and opportunities the rest of the way back to camp.

———◆◆◆———

A few moments of searching through our backpacks produced the necessary ingredients for supper. Now that I had a technique for lighting the stove, the meal promised to be done in no time. Tonight was stew and rice. Except for the fact that the wind was blowing more strongly and cooling the food more effectively, supper was about the same as the night before. This time the stove-lighting went so well that we decided to wait until after sunset to have our hot chocolate, even though that meant lighting the stove again.

I'm not sure how the subject got started, but as we were rubbing soap over our plates with our fingers, Jamie began to ask me about sexual arousal. What was sexual arousal anyway?

This turned my mind into a pretzel. At first all I could think of was other terms for it like "being turned on," "passion," or even "being horny." I tried all of these but got back the same puzzled look from my progeny.

"It is like being excited, but not exactly," my voice trailed off. "Boy! This is hard to explain! Maybe I'll have to settle for the old 'you'll just have to wait and find out for yourself' approach." After thinking for a minute more, other ideas began to trickle in. "It is kind of a good-bad feeling. Sort of like a tension—like when you have to go to the bathroom, only exciting at the same time. The difference is that sex feels good, so the tension feels good when it is over as long as you use right ways to deal with it.

"One of the tough things about adolescence is that sexual arousal seems to be popping up all over the place and with it come erections—you know, when your penis gets hard. It used to really embarrass me to ride in a bus because the vibrations often made me get an erection. When I got off the bus, I would have to walk and hold something in front of me until I was back to normal. All that time I kept hoping that no one would notice."

Jamie laughed, a nervous little laugh, as this was not a situation that he was looking forward to.

"As you get older, your body settles back down to a more reasonable level, but during teenage years almost everything causes an erection. Most embarrassing.

"Even at night there are erections; one about every ninety minutes to be precise. Often you wake up in the morning with an erection, and then you can't go to the bathroom until it goes down. Very annoying, if you really have to go. Some of these nighttime erections cause nocturnal emissions. That is an ejaculation of semen that happens when you are asleep. You wake up and your pajamas are all sticky. It sort of feels like you wet the bed, but there is a lot less liquid and it is sticky.

"I remember my first nocturnal emission. I woke up and right away took a sample out to my laboratory to look at under my microscope to see if I could see sperm swimming."

"Did you find any?"

"No! I was disappointed. Maybe I hadn't developed any yet, or I needed to stain them to make them visible. I'm not sure. I had twelve hundred times magnification, so that should have revealed something. I was sort of disappointed.

"Almost all boys also have self-assisted ejaculations. This used to be called *masturbation* as we talked about this afternoon, but now it is often called *self-stimulation*. Most children discover, about the time that they don't need to wear diapers, that rubbing their genitals feels good. Most seem to 'forget' about it until they are in their early teens. Almost all boys rediscover the sensation.

"There are many slang terms for self-stimulation as well." I went over the fifteen or twenty that I knew, then used the opportunity to explain some things about sexual humor.

"There are a lot of jokes about self-stimulation and other sexual subjects among boys. In fact, sexual things are one of their favorite things to make jokes about. One of the most common is using words with two meanings—one of them sexual, the other not. For instance, a few years ago when it rained so hard and there were so many rock slides on the coast there was a bumper sticker that said 'Malibu Get Your Rocks Off' which, as you can tell from the words we just went over about self-stimulation, has two meanings."

Jamie stuck up his nose. "That is dumb!" he said.

"Well, there are a lot of them like that. Some are funnier than others. Some are very funny. Many of them ignore or put down someone's value which is my objection."

"You might not think so to hear about it, but self-stimulation is a very controversial subject among Christians. There are lots of books written about what the Bible says on the topic. If you want, I can give you several to read. It is strange that this is such a big issue, since the Bible seems to ignore the topic altogether. If it was all that important, it seems to me that there should be at least one verse devoted to the subject. What is clear from both the Bible and the experience of self-stimulation is that it is a long way from the ideal sexual arrangement. God made sex for married, committed men and women to enjoy together. Anything less is basically unsatisfactory.

"That is not what you learn from most movies, books, magazines, or people. The general consensus is 'anything for fun.' Some people add 'as long as it doesn't hurt anyone,' but I guess they mean 'as long as it doesn't cause physical injury,' because a lot of people keep turning up hurt. Another favorite principle is 'anything goes between consenting adults.' This means that as long as two or more adults agree, they can do whatever they want to each other, whether people get hurt or not. Under this 'anything for fun' idea some people have sex with animals, objects, and even dead bodies like we discovered in the Bible study this morning."

"That is disgusting!" Jamie declared emphatically.

"You got it!" I said. "Sex gets used for lots of things it wasn't intended to do, like expressing hatred, personal power, or controlling and humiliating others through rape or child abuse."

As we packed our utensils away for the night we were silent, contemplating the disasters brought to light in the form of sexuality. It seems to be a common way for a person's defects to come to the surface.

"Jamie," I said, breaking the silence, "we need to talk about homosexuality. I have noticed that you and your friends have already been talking about it for a couple of years. I heard someone say a few weeks ago that he wasn't a 'homo,' but he would rather be friends with boys than girls."

Jamie didn't recall the conversation, but soon remembered others. "Yes," he said, "if you want to 'crumb' on someone you call them a 'homo' or a 'fag,' something like that."

"When boys are growing up, it is easier for them to relate to similar sorts of people, like other boys, than it is with different sorts of people, like girls. Sometime, usually around junior high age, society (which in this case is made up of the boys themselves) starts to put on a lot of pressure to force boys to be attracted to girls. Organized team sports are one of the main places where this is done. Part of it, at least, is to be sure that when sexuality develops boys will aim it at girls. That is precisely what most of them do. Homosexuals aim their sexuality at their same sex. There are both male and female homosexuals."

Once again we took some time to explore the common names for various forms of same sex preference.

"There is much that you can study and learn about homosexuality, Jamie, but for now I will say one thing—homosexuality is not God's ideal for us and we need to pursue, and help others pursue, God's ideal. Anything less causes people damage."

————◆◆◆————

After putting our trash in the little fire grate, where Bonnie and Clyde could not reach it, we began preparing to go to the west end for sunset. Jamie carried the flashlight while I had the camera. The view had been so magnificent the night before that it was worth a picture. Sunset photos have a way of seeming nice when you take them, but end up in a pile someplace where they get the occasional comment, "You can't tell it from this picture, but it was a magnificent sunset." We now have four more pictures in our sunset pile.

Once again our jackets felt good in the face of a brisk westerly breeze. It warmed my heart as well to put my arm around my son's shoulders as we walked together. It was time to personalize all of our talks for Jamie. After all, he wasn't just a general sort of human specimen entering adolescence, he was an individual with special characteristics that would make him unique as well.

About the time we reached the garbage pile left by the Chumash Indians, we simultaneously reached a lull in the conversation. Perhaps it was the idea of those early people eating shellfish and watching the sunset here only centuries ago that inspired the silence, but neither of us spoke until we reached the south facing cliffs and listened to the surf crashing far below.

"When you were born, your mother and I tried our best to be sure that everything was as close to right as we could make it. Like I told you, neither one of us had learned much about expressing our feelings, so we trained you as we thought best, which included being somewhat passive and not expressing anger. By the time your brother came along, we were much freer about expressing ourselves. As you can see, it is easier for him to be 'pushy' or assertive about expressing how he feels.

"When you boys got to school, we found, to our surprise, that both of you would rather do nothing than chance making a mistake. We had to work with you for several years to teach you that it is all right to make mistakes as long as you are trying. Do you remember how we would drop you off at school and say 'make some good mistakes today' as we left?"

Jamie nodded. He could remember that all right. At first it had taken some time to understand about "good mistakes." These mistakes, he came to find out, were signs that he was learning by challenging himself to something hard enough that he could not be sure of the outcome. Telling his parents about those mistakes was rewarded with smiles, cheers, and lots of encouragement. Still, given the choice between a mistake and no mistake he would always prefer no mistake.

"The secret of making it through adolescence is being comfortable with making lots of mistakes, like saying things even if they turn out later to be the wrong thing to say. It is OK to think before you speak, but it is also important to speak up, especially with me.

"You know that I have always been very definite when I say no to you. That is because I always try to listen to you before I have to say no. Other people are not always that way. Many say no right away to kids, and you have to be very persistent to get them to listen to you at all." We went over the examples of three teachers who had shut him off in the past year without knowing what he meant. "You need to keep fighting for what is right and for your chance to be understood. I would be a good person to practice with. If you can be persistent with me, then I think that you can be persistent with just about anyone. With me you can practice until you get good at what is called *assertiveness.*"

Jamie contemplated the horizons opening up to him as we seated ourselves at the west end of Anacapa. He had a serious sort of smile, but elected not to say anything. For my part, it was clear that this particular point would take lots of regular encouragement, mostly at times when I wouldn't feel like doing so.

"It might not be easy," I said at last, "to get through the conflict with parents that comes with being a teen. You see, it is your job to grow up and be independent and think for yourself. Meanwhile it is our job to help you stay steady and responsible during this time of big emotional ups and downs. Those two things don't always go together smoothly.

"You did not come equipped with perfect parents either," I said with a smile.

"No!?" Jamie said, feigning shock and then breaking into a laugh. His hands went deep into his pockets, and he almost disappeared into his jacket as he leaned against me again.

"Your mother has trouble letting you try things on your own. She likes to protect you from the world as much as possible. Mothers do that very often because they love their children and don't want them to be hurt. This often leads to fights during teen years when the young want to leave the nest.

"It is hard to balance independence with responsibility. Most teens want more independence without more responsibility. Their parents say, 'When you are more responsible then we will give you more independence. If you make your bed without being told then you can stay out until eleven on Saturday night.' There is a built in tug-of-war that keeps most families on their toes, unless they don't care what their kids do.

"It is like that gull over there," I said, pointing to an adolescent gull on the very edge of the rock who had been spreading his wings in the wind, and trying to get airborne without moving away from his rock. While this was going on, an adult gull kept watch from a few feet away. "The teen gull wants to fly, but the adult knows that it is not ready yet."

We remembered back to another gull whose first flight this afternoon had ended in the ocean. The attending parent had been able to do little more than make a great deal of noise. "Sometimes," I added soberly, "young gulls can get themselves in more trouble trying to fly than their parents can get them out of." The picture was too vivid and Jamie huddled closer under my arm, while I hugged him.

"My problem is that I tend to withdraw and become passive whenever there is a conflict at home. For instance, I hate it when there are arguments at the dinner table about food. Especially, 'how much do I need to eat to get dessert' arguments. I want to take my food and go to another room. If things are not going smoothly, it is too easy for me to head for the shop or find some project that needs to be done just so I can keep out of it.

"Over the years, I have had to learn that running away from problems gets peace at the moment but keeps the problem going, to be endured again another day. I have to work at not being passive when things get unpleasant. If I am active, I will be available for you whenever there are unpleasant things you need to deal with. Perhaps you learned some of your passivity from me; if so, you might learn to fight it from me as well. In fact, we probably can learn from each other."

While we were talking, the sun had set and we headed back to the camp. There was still enough light to start the stove without using the flashlight. Soon we were enjoying hot chocolate and warm feelings as we finished settling in for the night.

Safely tucked in our sleeping bags with the flaps of the tent open, we watched the stars come out and listened to the gull calls fade while we talked about the universe above and the "prairie in the Pacific" down here.

10

DRIVE DEFENSIVELY
(Anacapa—Day 3)

T HE WIND HAD DIED DOWN during the night. Jamie was still sound asleep when I crawled out of the tent. The island was still as I passed Lawrence of Arabia's tent and headed up the hill. From the top the view spread out for miles; even the mainland was visible already. As the waves crashed on rocks hundreds of feet below, a great splashing started a few hundred yards from shore. A pod of over one hundred Pacific whitesided dolphins had found a school of fish. One second the water would be still and the next moment fish would be doing tail walks across the water everywhere. Then a huge group of dolphins would sail into the air, leaping and skipping through the fish. During the next hour, the pod circled the east end of the island and could be seen leaping and cavorting about a quarter of a mile away. Too bad Jamie was not up! This was quite a show.

When Jamie emerged from the tent, I headed back to camp. No sooner had we settled down to breakfast then the pristine quiet of the island with its gulls and fog horn was shattered by a Coast Guard helicopter. The primus stove was no longer a challenge, so our breakfast entertainment was seeing the gulls that had dive-bombed us the night before put in their place. The concrete pad that the gulls called their own was regarded by the Coast Guard as their landing pad. After three attempts, the orange and white striped craft gave up, and the gulls once again won claim to the pad due to their superior perseverance.

Striking camp took most of our attention for the next half hour. After all of the preparations we had made to go on this trip, it seemed that it should have taken longer to pack for our return. I had sort of an empty feeling as we placed the backpacks under the camp table. The adventure was almost over. Would this trip make a difference in our lives? Had I talked too much or not listened enough? What was going on in Jamie's mind? Carefully I checked over my list; almost everything had been covered. The main objective for today was to have fun so that the trip would end on a great note, but would this island allow us to have fun? Yesterday's frustrations when we were trying to get into the ocean rushed into my mind. Jamie's voice brought me back.

"Let's go up to the landing pad, Dad."

His interest and enthusiasm were catching. After carefully arranging our caps so that we had "beaks" in front of us and behind us, we headed up the hill towards the concrete pad. The ground was covered with feathers and guano. Near the top our noses confirmed that the gulls had maintained a commanding presence here for some time. The air was soon full of flapping gulls, even though there were very few juveniles near us. Talking was an effort over the racket, so we said very little except for an occasional "look out!" as a bird swooped in from the side.

Further down the trail, we skirted what looked like a Spanish-style church. This building housed the ranger's water tank. Passing boats, it seems, used to use the water tank for shooting practice. Bullet holes were depleting the scarce water.

Someone struck on the idea of building a church-like structure over the tank, and there have been no bullet holes since.

——◆◆——

As we walked, Jamie consulted his list and found one last question.

"What do you do about your enemies—you know, kids that don't like you and want to pick fights?"

Part of both his uncertainty and fear was there because he had never been in a fight, and so had no experience to draw from in this matter. This, I assured him, meant that he had good skills in settling arguments with words instead of fists. We discussed the times he had talked his way out of, or walked away from, tight spots.

"What if someone attacks you?" he asked.

"That is a much harder question. I can remember being attacked a couple of times."

"Like when the kid pulled a knife on you?" he asked and I nodded. "What did you do then?" He pressed for more. Although he knew the story, he still wanted something he could use.

"Well, I was walking out of church when this street kid pulled a knife on me. He was very close and said that he was going to stab me and I believed him. Before he could move, I jumped on him and we rolled into the street where he landed on top of the knife with me on top of him. Amazingly neither one of us got cut, and I jumped up and got out of there as fast as I could go. It was very scary."

"Did you get in any other fights?"

"There were several times when someone was beating up on my little brother that I got into the fight. It would make me really mad when anyone was mean to him. I did some pretty mean things to him sometimes myself and always was very sorry afterward.

"The last fight I was in was when a big kid was fighting with Uncle Tim and I got in the middle to break it up. Uncle Tim was on one side punching me, and the other kid was on the other side punching me.

"In high school there were several boys who threatened to beat up me or my brother after school. We would walk home together very fast for a few weeks when that happened. Solomon said, 'If a man is alone, an assailant may overpower him, but two can resist.' That is part of why it is good to have friends."

"I get scared about getting in a fight," Jamie said at last. "I have never been in a fight, and I don't think I'd be very good at it." Looking down on this gentle, cautious boy, I couldn't help thinking that he was right.

"Hey!" shouted Jamie suddenly as we approached the fog-horn fence. The gulls at this end of the island had a new defense. "That gull pooped on me!" Just then one tried the same technique on me. We set off back down the hill at a brisk pace, leaving that end of the island unexplored.

"We got out of there fast," Jamie said as we rounded the bend at the bottom of the hill.

"Yes," I said. "Sometimes it is better to run than to fight."

Jamie wiped his arm ruefully. "Did they get you?" he asked grinning suddenly.

"No such luck!"

"It's a good thing you had a cap or they might have hit your bald spot." The thought of gulls hitting such a target clearly amused him as he continued down the hill. For my part I was glad for my cap.

When we were safely out of range, I returned to our topic. "You know, Jamie, Jesus has a very difficult teaching on fighting. He said that if someone strikes you on one cheek you should turn the other cheek also. That sounds a lot like 'don't fight back' to me. Christians have argued over that for a long time. Some say that it means don't be quarrelsome or easily provoked into a fight. Others say it means don't fight at all. As you know, I am a pacifist which means that I don't believe in fighting and hurting or killing other people. Still I don't know what I would do if I were stuck in a situation where I had to kill or be killed. I pray that I will never find out. The whole idea is that I don't want any people hurt.

"It makes a difference whether you are fighting to protect or to attack. In the Garden of Eden God told us to protect and tend the earth. Men are to be protectors. If someone tried to hurt my family and the only way to stop them was to hurt them, I'm sure I would do it. I would rather see one person hurt than two or more people hurt. I would rather see a guilty person hurt than an innocent one. I would not want to kill anyone. Jesus' teaching on turning the other cheek is a hard one, and you will have to decide for yourself how to live with it. I can't be brave or spiritual with your life or body for you."

Silence reigned for a while, and I knew that these words would not be lost even though the growth would take some time.

We took a while to explore the nature center that housed the basic exhibits for the day trip visitors to Anacapa. But since we turned up very little that was new to us except for the history of the lighthouse, we were soon outside again.

The area outside the nature center was jammed with people. There must have been thirty or forty of them noisily opening coolers and milling about. The boat had arrived and this group dragged up their food and beer and sat down to picnic. Except for three or four people they stayed jammed together there for the rest of the day. They seemed oblivious to the island around them. Each time we passed the nature center they were eating, drinking, talking, yelling at their kids, and lining up in front of the outhouses.

"Let's go diving," Jamie said, pointing toward the landing area. That sure sounded like fun, and I told him so. We took the long way there, stopping by camp to pick up our backpacks and carry them with us so that we would be ready to leave on the afternoon boat. As we walked, Jamie brought us back to the topic. "What happens if you get into a fight?"

"Besides being scared?"

"Yeah!"

"Usually you don't just get into a fight. You see trouble coming ahead of time, even if it is only a few seconds. Then you have to make two quick and important decisions. First, do the persons intend harm, or are they only trying to provoke a fight? Those are two different things. We should try to avoid being easily provoked and use our heads to stay calm.

"Second, if they do intend to harm you, regardless of what you do, then decide whether you can or should escape. If you can't escape, fight suddenly and as hard as you can, then run. Fighting is like jumping off a diving board. If you do it halfway, you really get hurt. So if you are going to hit, then hit or kick hard enough to disable your opponent. Give it everything you have, then get out of there to someplace safe and call the authorities. The only reason to fight is to allow yourself or someone else to get to safety."

"You mean hurt them enough so they can't chase you and then get away?" Jamie asked, more as a way to summarize than as a question.

"Yes. That is what your mother learned in her rape prevention, self-defense course." We talked about ways in which one could disable an attacker for a while, then I said, "There are four parts to being strong—brains to plan and avoid trouble; speed of action to be ahead of your opponent; skill and practice at the techniques that you use; and power that is made up of strength and endurance. Remember that there will always be someone who has more fighting ability than you have. You will need to use what you have most of and plan to keep away from trouble." Just then we rounded the corner to the landing.

———⊷•⊶———

"Getting in the water around here isn't easy, is it?" Jamie remarked when we found the landing area closed off again.

This time the wait was a short one while the park service removed some asbestos debris that had been left during World War II to pollute the island.

We watched with fascination as a large seal cruised by in the cove, wishing all the while that we were in the water for a close look at such a magnificent swimmer. The way was soon clear, however, and in no time we were in our wet suits climbing down the ladder into the clear cold Pacific.

In a few kicks of our fins, the bottom fell away from twenty to thirty-five feet deep. Still, we could see everything below us. Around us there were schools of bait fish. Before long we were finding our way through fifty-foot tall kelp packed wall-to-wall on the surface. A quick bend of our waists and we sailed weightlessly fifteen feet below the canopy and in between the nicely spaced, gentle giants of this undersea forest.

As we crossed the main bay, we came across a strange school of fish. What made this strange was that the school was made up of all different types of fish. We stopped for a look. It was a fish cleaning station. Fish would wait for their turn to have a slender, cigar-shaped senorita wrasse nibble the parasites out of their mouths and bodies.

Jamie was more interested in a large black fish with a broad red stripe on its side that resembled the markings of the Coast Guard helicopter. This sheepshead fish, which he spotted poking around a small reef, had the strange history of starting out as a nice pink female and after a few years changing to a black and red male. Watching him, I mused that he had no excuse for not understanding the female of his species. How would humans behave if we developed that way?

Talking with a snorkel in your mouth and face in the water is, to say the least, not easy. I decided that I would have to wait for the boat trip back before discussing these musings with the little fellow holding on to my shoulder with one hand and pointing with the other. After exploring for a while more, I suddenly found myself looking up at a pair of flippers that could only be there if Jamie's head was well out of the water.

"Dad, I'm cold! Can we go in?" A quick glance at my watch indicated that forty minutes had elapsed since we slipped in. After a quick check for boat traffic, we headed back. We passed a fledgling gull that had jumped off the cliffs above before it could fly. It climbed onto a rock just in time for a wave to knock it off again. We had watched it fall yesterday. At first an adult gull flew down and floated around with it but in less than an hour the young bird was on its own. We had fantasies of rescuing it, but even after a day in the ocean the bird and its razor beak were much faster than either of us. We were soon glad to be out of the water and in the sunshine.

As we got out of our insulated wet suits, one of the lady rangers, in her bathing suit, jumped into the water and swam around. Finally, she swam out to a boat anchored about half again as far as we had explored.

"Doesn't she get cold?" Jamie put words to the thoughts of many.

"I get cold just watching her," said Lawrence of Arabia, who stood near us.

"How did your patch hold?" I asked, remembering how two hours of pumping yesterday had yielded a pancake instead of a raft.

His companion smiled. "We took the raft to the end of the island this morning. I hope you don't mind. We used your weight belt to hold down the patch," she said.

"Feel free to use it if you like," Lawrence said warmly.

"That sounds great, but we go back today," I answered. "We're going to try to get in another dive when we warm up."

"Look! She is coming back!" Jamie said from his vantage point on the wall, and sure enough the ranger was swimming back from the boat. Boy! It felt good to sit in the sun!

We watched for a while as the rangers loaded more garbage onto their boat. Then, when the coast was clear, we suited up and headed back down the ladders for another swim.

This dive started much like the other one except that we headed across the cove to the sunlit side where we knew the visibility would be best. Suddenly we both began pointing excitedly as a large bat ray "flew" by fifteen feet below us, its four-foot wings slowly moving up and down at the tips, propelling its diamond-shaped body gracefully through the water. This was great! Jamie had never seen one before, so we had a quick conference at the surface before continuing.

We explored the mouth of a sea cave that was dark and spooky and more exciting than interesting. With most of the Pacific Ocean still left to explore, we saw the crowd with their ice chest gathering on the dock and realized that it was time to get dressed for the trip home. We found ourselves eager to get out and get dry and warm.

In minutes we were heading toward the boat. As we boarded, we could hear the sound of schools of fish jumping. It was like showers of rain to both the eye and ear. We watched as a brown pelican would swoop low over the water and a whole school would jump together as the bird passed over or splashed in with its beak pouch bulging.

Careful watching soon identified several black, long necked cormorants who were diving and fishing beyond the cove. They were a vision of grace and form compared with the crash dives of the pelicans. Jamie liked to watch for cormorants, enjoying the sense of mastery that comes from being able to find and name things in nature.

"Look, Dad, is that a cormorant with a short neck?" he said pointing to a smaller black bird with a red beak.

Now it was my turn to be excited. "No, that is a black oystercatcher. I have been looking for one all trip!"

Somehow, seeing that oystercatcher seemed to make the trip complete for me. Jamie was decidedly restless and ready to head for home. He began to go over the stories he had to tell, as we raised anchor and headed for the California coast. The knowledge and history were now in his hands, the rite of passage was complete. The great father-and-son trip to find out about puberty was over.

COMING HOME
A MAN

I T TOOK NO TIME AT ALL to be back to life as usual in the
Wilder household. I was back to work the next day, where
windy islands seemed oh, so far away. There was garbage to
take out and grass to mow. The only signs of the trip were the
borrowed backpacks and stove waiting to be returned to their
owner. In a few days even those traces were gone.

The whole trip, including the food we took along, had cost
about eighty dollars, less than the going rate for one hour of
psychotherapy. Even if all that came of it were the memories of
an enjoyable adventure, it was a worthwhile investment. Somehow, I expected that there would be more dividends from
those three days, and I was not disappointed. Jamie was becoming a man.

Every so often, events took place to indicate that the
Anacapa trip had not been completely forgotten. A few weeks
after we returned from the island Jamie went to his mother and
asked her how she had felt about her menarche. He was puzzled when Mom didn't seem to know what he was talking

about. "You know, Mom, your menarche is when you have your first menstruation. Isn't that what it is called?"

Well, Mom didn't know the word *menarche*, and we had quite a few chuckles about it. Mom asked several of her friends and they hadn't heard of it either. One of our friends (Cathy of the cholla cactus and chowder calamity) heard the story, and she laughed at me. In my self-satisfied way I had been pronouncing *menarche* as "men-arch" when it should rhyme with monarchy and be pronounced "men-are-key." Now we had two funny stories to laugh about.

Soon after this, we heard an excited shout from the shower one evening. "Hey, Mom and Dad, I think I've got a pubic hair! Do you want to see it?" I was rather flustered. The enthusiasm was unmistakable but examining for sprouting hairs had not figured in my idea of a father's role. Still this was a major event and not to be squelched. My wife uttered, "That's nice!" and headed toward the bedroom.

"Do you want to see it, Mom?" He had heard the footsteps.

"No, thank you." The bedroom door closed, and I was on my own.

"Hey, Dad," he said, emerging from the bathroom, "I think I'm getting a pubic hair. Do you want to see it?"

"Say, that's exciting!" I said, "Adolescence is on its way! But it is good enough for me to know you are coming along. Keeping track of those hairs is your private business. I'll watch for the ones on your upper lip."

"Okay!" he said, and galloped off to his bedroom full of smiles and enthusiasm. For my part, I sank into a chair to contemplate this event.

<hr/>

It gives us—as parents—a good feeling to see eagerness and enthusiasm in our children. This is especially true when they are excited by a challenge like doing their math homework, or going to summer school, or other unlikely events. Since adolescence was my all-time worst part of life, it feels good to me to watch my kids anticipate this phase with all its changes.

One summer afternoon Jamie came up behind me and leaned on the couch. "With your great psychological mind, tell me again what kids do in high school. In junior high they use their power on each other. What about high school?"

"In junior high they use their power on each other, and in high school they use it on adults," I answered.

"What if they use their power on adults and they win?" He looked quite concerned. He had recently visited a home dominated by an out-of-control teenage boy, so I answered, "Then chaos reigns supreme."

At this he began to nervously circle the couch. "You won't let me win when I get to high school, will you?" he said, checking the skin between his fingers while he walked.

"What do you think?" I said smiling.

"I don't think you like chaos."

"The way with power around here is to learn to use it well. If you make a mess, you clean it up."

He perched over the back of the couch again. "That is the way it has been all my life." I rumpled his hair and he was gone.

I sensed that Jamie was feeling fear of being out of control. It was most important to him that I was not afraid of his power. We had made another step toward establishing that he did not need to be afraid of his own power, since it was not overwhelming to me. He could still make his mistakes while learning. With power comes responsibility. This was not something new, simply an outgrowth of what he had already experienced, only on a more grandiose scale.

While he and his brother played catch outside, I mused over some of the components of personal power. Logic is one useful kind of power, especially when it is combined with knowledge. Arguing is one sign of teens testing this part of their power. It seems that they should win if they are right, so perhaps I had overstated that chaos business.

Strong feelings are another part of power. Someone who gets very angry, sad, or excited, among other emotions, can have a big influence on the rest of the family. Strong feelings should always be respected even if they cannot always prevail.

Abilities and experience are also components of personal power. When used wisely, the whole family, as well as the individual, can appreciate the impact of a teen's abilities. There are also negative abilities, like being able to intimidate others, that may need to be challenged or channeled. The purpose of a family is to help the members benefit separately and corporately from these tools.

Possessions, personality, and personal attractiveness also provide teens with power. As always, those who do not realize that they have power are the most hazardous. They will use their personal power carelessly and indiscriminately to the detriment of themselves, their friends, and family.

Certainly then, the goal cannot be to keep teens powerless all the time. Neither does it do us or them any good to let them dominate. Winning all the time is bad. It does not matter who is winning all the time—winning all the time is unhealthy.

I rarely resort to giving a direct parental "no" because having power does not need to be a win-or-lose situation. Most of the time a little creativity will make a situation where everyone can win. Something is wrong if you face very many win-or-lose situations a month. (Hint—it is probably not the children.)

Parents have the job of giving power gradually to their children. If you move too slowly, they will wrestle it from you. Equally bad is giving power too soon. I remember one call that came into my office a while ago. The parents said their daughter was staying out too late, wearing makeup and jewelry that they did not approve of, and bossing everyone around. Her parents did not like her friends. They were not even sure that they could get her to agree to come in to see me. "How old is she?" I asked. "She is five, almost six," they said. You know, they never did talk her into coming in to see me! Children will almost always take any power that is given to them but rarely are able to use parental power well.

Children need to have power and responsibility over their own life as soon as they can handle each step. They do not need power or responsibility for their parents' lives unless the parents become senile.

But let's get back to the story. The next morning over breakfast I brought up the topic of power. I explained to Jamie that what I told him was not completely right. "It is important for everyone to win sometimes. Power comes from being right or having strong feelings about something. You would want to win if you were right, wouldn't you?"

"That would be good," he said and poured the milk.

"It is rotten if one person wins all the time. Suppose that I always used my power and what your mom wanted or what you wanted did not count at all. That would be a lousy way to live." He agreed and poured the sugar—more on the table than in the bowl. "I think that when we do things right, all of us can win and get what is important to us, like when you can stay with a friend and do not have to go on some boring errand with your mom or me. It won't always work that way, but it is good to try.

"Does that make sense?" I asked.

"Sure," he said, shoveling in the cereal.

"Good! Then I can go back to thinking I am very wise." All that got was a snort as he returned to his breakfast. His fears had been faced yesterday and for now he was reassured that I was not afraid of his power. Perhaps he heard that I respected his power as well, but the real message will be in the way I behave in the situation.

Have you ever noticed that some weeks are longer than others? It had been what could only be labeled as a "moody week" for Jamie. Nothing suited him. He dragged his feet when asked to hurry and pestered us when we did not drop everything to attend his interests. He cried about his glasses and was mad about his meals. It was a week of dubious quality. Sunday afternoon we all went to the beach. He did not like sand castles, and the "rad" waves that attracted his brother with the boogie board hardly got a glance. Jamie simply flopped on the blanket and lay there.

After he had baked his brain for two hours, I pulled up a chair and primed him with a soft drink. "Have you noticed that you have had a lot of feelings this week?" I asked. "You have been upset quite often and more strongly than usual, I think."

"I hadn't until you mentioned it," he said.

"Welcome to adolescence, old boy! The ride has started."

He smiled and rolled over. About a half hour later he said, "I think I'll go join the others." Sand castles were interesting again—for a while.

One day Kitty came over to me and said, "I think it is time for Jamie to have some deodorant of his own. He is starting to sweat like a teenager." She is much better at observing things than I. We wondered how to make this event as interesting as possible so we offered him the option of going to the store and picking out any brand he wanted or having one of the same brand I use. He chose the latter and was soon presented with a unit of his own. With a smile on his face he headed toward his room. Moments later, he charged back out, deodorant lifted high, and announced proudly, "When I am done with this deodorant I am going to have it bronzed and keep it forever!"

Now that is enthusiasm! The real surprise came from Rami, however. Jamie had just developed his very first blemish and was ruefully examining this aspect of puberty. As we sat around the supper table discussing this development, Jamie was receiving sympathy from both his parents when Rami exclaimed, "Wow! A zit! I can't wait until I have a zit!" Turning to his mother he said, "Do you think that I will ever get a zit?" He seemed genuinely worried that this landmark of development would pass him by.

"Oh, yes!" said Mom. "Both your father and I had them,

and we can practically guarantee some for you."

"I can hardly wait! Just think! A zit! Can I see it?"

Jamie hid the exhibit and tried to slump under the table. He clearly did not share his brother's views on blemishes.

"You might not feel that way when you have one," his mother cautioned.

"Yeah!" said Jamie.

Once we quit laughing, our meal resumed.

By now I was quite pleased with the way the relationship with my sons was progressing. Perhaps I was becoming too confident about the results of the Anacapa trip and the improvement of father-son relations, but it wasn't long before reality poked its head in the door.

As you may recall, part of the Anacapa trip was to serve as a preparation for a full-scale backpack trip in the High Sierras that summer. After our practice on the island with stoves and the backpacks themselves, we hoped to know what we were doing when our church group headed for twelve thousand feet. Rami, the most athletic among us, benefited from our experience but didn't require as much practice.

The trip was magnificent. We very nearly made it to the top of Mount Langley. We stopped at about the twelve-thousand-eight-hundred-foot level near a series of rock piles that housed dozens of furry, overgrown squirrels called *marmots*. We named this spot "Marmot Condominium." There was a lot of trust and camaraderie between the backpackers by the time we headed back to civilization. We left camp saying, "This year the marmot condos, next year Mount Langley." Looking at nature inspires in us some of the respect that God deserves.

In our car pool down the mountain and back across the Mojave Desert, there was lots of time to talk. We reminisced about our experiences on the backpack trip. Some of us older folk talked about trips our families had taken when we were children. Rami, who likes to hear stories, asked us about whether we had boyfriends or girlfriends when we were his age. We all said yes, but not one of us would have admitted it when we were Rami's age. The suggestion that they might learn from our mistakes was greeted with Jamie's protest. "But, Dad, that was when you were young. Girls have changed! These are the eighties!"

That caught me a little off guard. Somehow I was expecting a little more respect and admiration about my experience and astute observations about the nature of boy-girl interactions. It seemed independence was here sooner than anticipated. I made mental notes to not try to push my experience on my sons and to remember to bring this up in thirty years or so for some good chuckles.

------◆◆◆------

Laughter in a family is great. It is the emotional lubricant that helps us slip through those hard times. There are very few things that produce as nice a sense of relief as being able to laugh at ourselves. It is particularly helpful to be able to laugh at being wrong, dumb, or awkward at those times when we are each of those (and everyone is at some time or another). But I'm talking about that genuine, amused, relaxed laugh that comes with enjoyment, not the tense laugh in response to shame or put-downs.

I like to tease and laugh, but it is most important that the other person (if this joke is on them) is genuinely enjoying the experience. I make sure that enough of the jokes are on me to stay balanced. If the other person is sensitive about the subject, it is not time to laugh about it yet. I must be sure that they feel very understood first. That is why many things are not funny until later for the person involved, so be prepared to wait sometimes.

Fathers, it seems, are particularly prone to laugh at others and tease in a way that hurts the feelings of their family. Many times there is even a put-down hidden in the joke. This is not funny, but the family will laugh anyway to cover their hurt.

"Sex," one missionary friend once told me, "is the funniest thing in the world. Nothing ever goes right." If you can laugh at yourself and the things that go wrong with your sex life and functions you are well on the road to self-acceptance.

Many parents tease their children about their boyfriends or girlfriends. Kitty announced some time ago that when our boys got old enough to have girlfriends she would not tease them about it. She looked at me severely, no doubt thinking about my tendency to have a little fun with anything available, and inquired about my intentions. She had a very good point and a very good plan. As a result, when our offspring asked the first questions about whether we had liked anyone in fourth grade, a rather matter-of-fact conversation took place. These talks were greeted with great interest and, slowly, preferences for certain girls began to emerge.

This didn't mean that we couldn't have some fun and laugh. At first, all girls were awful. When they told of the "terrible" things that happened, like chasing or being chased all around the playground by some certain girl, I'd go right along with them. First I'd put on my saddest face, slowly shake my head back and forth, and proclaim that surely this was the saddest day in the history of humankind. They would roar with laughter. Soon they were full of such stories. Any suggestion, usually by Mom, that they liked this attention from girls brought forth emphatic denials and choruses of "We hate girls."

In time things changed some, and one day Jamie came to ask, "Dad, how do you talk to a girl?"

"In English," did not seem to satisfy, so I reminded him that for over a year he had been talking to a girl in the neighborhood who was part of the group of kids going in and out of our house at any given moment. Jamie was getting impatient now, clearly thinking his dad wasn't up to understanding this problem.

"I mean, how do you talk to a special girl?" he said, shuffling his feet.

"You talk to her in the same way."

"No," he said, "that won't work. This girl is different—special."

"Well, your feelings about her may be special, but talking to her is done the same way as you would talk to anyone."

"How is that, Dad?"

"Son, just imagine that she is a human being." A faint smile greeted this remark. "Find out about her and her interests, family, and opinions. Tell her about yourself." We chatted for a while on the usual form of interactions between Jamie and his friends.

After a satisfying talk, Jamie leaned on the counter and returned to the original theme. He hopped from one foot to the other and asked, "Dad, are you sure that there isn't anything you have forgotten to tell me about talking to girls?" Good advice and friendly conversation were fine, but this was a *special* girl and he was still nervous. I leaned over and in a low voice said, "Well, there is the myth about the shoes." Then I went back to my work.

"What about the shoes?" said Jamie, hopping back and forth more noticeably.

I put aside my project and leaned over the opposite side of the counter. After looking around to be sure we were alone, I said quietly. "There is a belief among boys, which has been around for some time, that girls can make your shoes disappear. I first heard about it when I was a boy, but it is still believed in many places. The myth is that if you talk to a girl for too long—zap—the shoes are gone!" Puzzlement and disbelief were spreading over the young face that I watched intently.

"Now it simply isn't true, but if you watch boys while they talk to girls, you can pick out the ones who believe this myth because they nervously keep an eye on their shoes whenever they talk to girls. Just watch for it at school, you will see! I tell you though, it is just a myth. No matter how nervous you get, girls cannot 'zap' your shoes!"

"Dad!"

We stood there grinning at each other for a few seconds,

then he took off for the front yard, where the group of neighborhood kids were gathering for either an assault on our living room or a game of some kind.

How the relationship with that special girl turned out is fascinating as well—but that is Jamie's story.

About a year later, Jamie came bouncing into the kitchen where Kitty and I were talking. It was after his bedtime and so it was a surprise to see him.

"Dad," he said, hopping up and down excitedly, "Rami just asked me how to talk to girls. It is time to tell him the myth about the shoes! Come on!" With that he sailed back to the bedroom. It had been an extraordinarily bad day, so I took a few minutes to prepare for the story, including looking over my notes.

When I arrived in the bedroom, Jamie climbed halfway up the top bunk to witness this event. Rami sat up.

"I understand that you want to know how to talk to girls."

"Yeah!"

"Tell him about the shoes," said a voice at my elbow.

"I want to know what you talk to them about and stuff."

"Well, you can talk to them about themselves, their families, school, things you are interested in like baseball. Some girls like baseball. You would have it made with one of them.

"What do you talk about with your friend Julie across the street? She is a girl."

"Same example, Dad!" said the voice at my elbow.

"Call me boring!" I replied.

"I don't know," said Rami, looking pensive. "I never thought about it."

"Tell him about the shoes!"

"There is a myth about shoes that you should know if you are going to talk to girls. Do you know what a myth is?"

"It is a story that isn't true."

"Right!" And so Rami heard the myth.

When I finished Rami said, "You mean that I shouldn't look at my feet and just talk to the girl."

"That's it," I said.

Rami, who likes to sleep in those colorful beach-style shorts, put his hands in his pockets, looked down at his knees, and rocked back and forth. "Not like this."

"Yes," I said. "Just imagine that girls are people and talk to them like that."

"Same line, Dad!" Jamie said, laughing.

"That's right! Why do you suppose it took so long for me to come in here? I was reading over the story to be sure I got it right." With that I turned to go.

"Good night, boys. I love you."

"I love you too" came back in stereo.

QUESTIONS AND ANSWERS ABOUT THE STORY

1. Was it really as easy for you as it seems?

It is not easy for me to be a father. Sometimes I think that I should have written a book about being a husband. I would usually give myself an A as a husband, but this business of being a father is harder. It is easy to do almost nothing at all with my children and still feel that I am a good father if I growl a bit and say, "Do what your mother tells you." Overall I have been a C+ father, but I'm working toward a B+.

It is probably easier for me to talk about personal matters than it is for most people. I have had training in sex therapy. That alone probably makes me more relaxed with sexuality than most folks. What that means is I got over my embarrassment with someone other than my own children. Even so, it wasn't with my clients that I worked through most of the embarrassment, it was with Kitty. Something so personal should be first discussed with your partner. It is a safe guess that if you don't practice getting over your discomfort by talking about sex with the person who shares your sexual activity with you, it will be embarrassing to talk to anyone else about something quite so intimate.

I remember the first time that Kitty and I went to hear Walter Trobisch speak. What impressed me most was that he would pause every few minutes and say, "Does that make you feel uncomfortable?" The truth was that hearing him use words I could barely slip past my lips did make me uncomfortable! My hands were cold and I would hardly glance at Kitty for fear that the whole audience (who doubtlessly had come to stare at us) would know something about our problems or pleasures.

Years of talking with Kitty, and later clients, have changed me considerably. Still, whenever the topic comes up for the first time with someone, the old discomfort makes a short appearance and I say, "What is this problem you are having with errrr ... sex?" Then remembering Walter, I say, "Isn't this uncomfortable to talk about?" And with a round of nervous laughter we are off.

Getting back to the difficulty level of this father-and-son adventure, the hardest part was overcoming my own passivity and inclination to stay uninvolved. After all, when nothing is overtly going wrong, no problems to fix, no rules to enforce, no ways to feel powerful and be incredibly helpful, what is a father to do? Entering my son's room only reveals Jamie flopped on his bed sort of blinking at me. My great ideas for activities draw the response "Do we have to?" a lot. It was easier when he was two years old. In those days he wanted to get rides, be thrown in the air, spun around until I begged for mercy and dreamed of his bedtime.

These days it is easy to quit trying to stay involved and forget that these boys need me to help them become men. I have to force myself to stay involved, especially when that means learning how many José Canseco cards Topps printed, and what the rookie card is going for these days. What boys need is to know that *men*, and especially Dad, find them interesting.

For me that means learning the current market price for donuts between third and fourth periods at Washington Junior High. Even though I am usually interested in my sons, this kind of interest in their world seems unnatural and comes only with concentration and effort. For me, the real payoff comes when discussing the 300 percent markup on donuts becomes a short discussion on greed.

There is no way to be sure what ultimate results I'll get for all this effort. But Jamie does seem to be off to a good start, based on the reflections he wrote for this book. I hope that one day my sons will manifest a quiet confidence that God the Father is interested in them. Possibly they will be less driven to find some girl who will perform the miracle of finding them interesting. All I am sure of is that staying involved is difficult for me to do day after day.

2. What is childhood sexuality like?

Aside from the fact that by the age of two, children need to establish in their own minds whether they are boys or girls, most adults are completely unaware of the existence of sexuality in prepubescent children. There is a popular belief that sexuality only emerges at age thirteen or fourteen as if by magic. This is not true.

The biological sexual response develops with time but begins early. Boys have been born with erections. They continue to have this ability throughout childhood. Boys are able to have orgasms while still very young, although the ability to ejaculate develops around puberty. Girls are also orgasmic from a young age. Obviously, no experimental scientific studies exist on this subject (and we hope they never will). Yet, enough is known from the response of children to traumatic incidents to know that biology begins to function very young, certainly under two years of age.

Most children will discover the pleasure of touching their genitals in about the same way as they discover their toes or their tongue. This discovery usually occurs about the time that they are leaving diapers. The moment when parents unexpectedly face their son or daughter's new discovery is when most children receive their first major lesson on sexuality. It is a lesson that they will never consciously remember, yet never forget.

It is my guess that most parents handle the discovery of a penis or clitoris very differently from the discovery of toes. They don't coo or say, "This little piggy went to market," like the child heard with other discoveries!

Knowing that this event was coming, I prepared myself for my children's inevitable discovery. It got the same treatment as sticking your finger in your nose. We explained the names of the new body parts they had discovered along with their proper care. In the first place it was a private part not to be shown or touched in public—like the insides of their noses. We pointed out our example. Parents have these parts too, but we take care of them when we are alone.

The two parts of the message were privacy and special care. This message was repeated on several different occasions. So far the results have been most satisfactory. We were careful to avoid negative messages like: "Don't touch that! It is dirty!" or threats, "If you put your hand there again we will cut it off!" Which, it is sad to say, is the kind of message many children hear.

It was also helpful to teach them the right words for genitals and sexual activity. We told them that rubbing your genitals was called *masturbation* or *self-stimulation*, but we preferred the latter term. Some people refer to self-stimulation as *touching yourself* but that is rather vague, while the term *masturbation* stirs up all sorts of feelings for most people. We made sure to remind the boys after each discussion to keep these conversations within our own family.

Gender identity is another important part of sexuality that develops over time. In the first two years children learn that they are either boys or girls. From two to five years of age they learn how boys and girls act, what they play with, feel, and like. From six to nine is the time to learn that it is OK to be whatever you are. You become one of the boys or girls. Loyalty is demonstrated by not liking the other gender. Boys against girls is a common grade school development.

From nine to thirteen children learn a great deal about how to treat the opposite gender. The example of the same sex parent carries the greatest influence. Boys learn to treat women like Dad does, girls treat men like Mom does. Children can also switch and do the opposite of what their parents do when they are especially revolted by their parents' behavior.

Although it occurs at all ages, the years of thirteen to eighteen are particularly important for a child in learning if their gender identity is acceptable to the opposite sex. The most important factor is the treatment received from the opposite gender parent. If he or she is affirming and protective of their gender and sexuality, there is much less need for them to prove themselves through sexual activity.

3. What about your reluctance to say no? Doesn't a parent need to be strict and firm sometimes?

Yes, it is important to be firm. But just like flexing a muscle, being firm doesn't take long to give you a cramp. Parental firmness has been extensively explored in the writings of others.

While firmness is necessary, rigidity is almost never required. Parents should never be tough as a shortcut to teaching their children. Parents should never be understanding to avoid directing their children's choices. In general if you feel you are wasting your breath talking to someone, they are being rigid. If you feel understood but the answer didn't change, they are being firm.

Of course, the real fun starts when you try to convince a rigid person that they are being rigid and should change! Many families show up for family counseling because they face this problem. Extremely rigid people are in the category that the Bible calls *fools*. This topic could take a whole book but briefly consider the following points.

A fool can be described by any one of the following characteristics taken from Proverbs (an incomplete list):

Slanders family members or others (10:18)
Is short-tempered (12:16)
Brings trouble on his family (11:29)
Is lewd or has a "dirty mind or mouth" (10:23)
Is always right (12:15)

This is why some people, while appearing firm, are in constant conflict with their families. Their firmness does not come from wisdom but from a short temper or thinking themselves to be right. This kind of rigid thinking is not open to needed change and is a major affliction to family members.

Let us consider four arguments against being a rigid person. First, no one is always right. Believing you are always right (Prv 12:15) or too wise to need counsel (Prv 26:12) leads to acting foolish. We need to appreciate correction when we are wrong. "A reproof is felt by a man of discernment more than a hundred blows by a stupid man" (Prv 17:10).

Second, even if you are right, there are valid reasons to change decisions and punishments. The objective of discipline is teaching and helping children grow—not enforcing rules. Even God changes his mind. He is not rigid. We rightly look to God as a model of how to be fathers. Let us consider some examples of our Lord's technique.

Once there was a very wicked city called Nineveh and God sent a prophet named Jonah to announce their destruction. The king and people repented and God spared the city. This story shows us a change in consequences because God saw that his children were sorry.

Later on King David sinned, and God gave him a choice of three punishments. The punishment David chose was not yet completed when God changed his mind and lessened the severity (1 Chr 21:15). This case illustrates both giving the child a choice of consequences and a reduction of the severity of punishment at the parent's own initiative.

King Hezekiah was told by a prophet that he was about to die. This was not a punishment, nor are we told that Hezekiah had done anything wrong. The king asked God to live longer because he had always served God, and God changed his decision and granted the king fifteen more years (2 Kgs 20:5). We can learn from this story that it is acceptable to change our minds sometimes when we are asked to by our children.

An even more interesting story involves the evil King Ahab. He was told that he would die along with other consequences of his misdeeds. Ahab dressed himself for mourning and went around muttering to himself. He didn't even talk to God. All the same, God took notice and remitted part of the consequences simply because he noted a response in the right direction by Ahab. Ahab continued to be as bad as ever (1 Kgs 21:27-29).

Regrettably, some of us end up with little Ahabs. They seldom do what is right and often cause great harm to others. Sometimes a partially right response is all we see. The child doesn't even approach us with repentance. Still, we are free to respond to these partial and unsatisfactory changes. Being rigid prevents such change and paradoxically puts the rebellious child in control of the rigid parent's behavior.

These examples suggest that there is room for parents to be flexible in decisions and discipline in response to their children's behavior or the parent's observation that change would be merciful or helpful. Sometimes consequences should be moved to later or changed entirely. Notice that we are talking about parents that start with fair and predictable consequences. This is a very long way from being rigid on the one hand, or uninvolved on the other.

Third, rigid people usually rely on threats to motivate others. Threats are easy to identify. Their objective is to limit the choice or leave no choice to the person who hears them. Most threats start off with the words *if you* and end with something bad that will happen. Threats are always evil. No masculine man will use or imply threats. Rigid people, however, seek control through threats in order to confine the actions of others to their rigid guidelines.

Those who think this view extreme might be interested to note that Jesus never threatened anyone (1 Pt 2:22-23). Further, since threats are based on fear and Jesus operated in love, it would make no sense for him to wish to be the source of fear. Threats are always the friends of demons. Demons like fear and threats. Threats give them a chance to make their evil power available. Jesus, on the other hand, offered people a choice. In fact, his followers believe that they will be given a choice no matter how threatening the situation (1 Cor 10:13).

Many people who would not think of using threats in any other context find them necessary for "training" children. Threats, like all abuses of power, get faster reactions than providing choices. Using threats to achieve good purposes is like using a gun to get your child to kiss you. If you mix threats with sound morals, you are still double minded and can expect an unstable family for all your trouble (Jas 1:8, 26; 3:9-10).

Fourth, rigid control leads to excessive punishment. Consider the following proverbs:

Like a fluttering sparrow or a daring swallow, groundless abuse gets nowhere. **Proverbs 26:2**

Again, to punish the righteous is not good and it is wrong to inflict blows on men of noble mind. **Proverbs 17:26**

In the life of the downtrodden every day is wretched.
Proverbs 15:15

So you see, a little ancient wisdom can go a long way towards making us more firm and flexible. By contrast, being rigid leads to misery for the fool who is rigid and those around him or her. They become tyrants instead of parents. Unfortunately there are more tyrants sitting in deacons' row on Sunday than there are in world governments.

4. Is it a good idea to tell a child so much about yourself?

Our children will try to use our example, whether good or bad, to help them live their lives. What problem do you have that you don't expect your child will need help facing? Let them benefit from our experience if they will.

Suppressing important information about yourself makes your motives confusing to your children. If they can understand your history, then they can better explain your behavior. For instance, knowing about the date rape of my grandmother helped me understand why my mother became cool towards me when I became an adolescent boy. By using that history my father helped me to avoid feeling rejected by my mother's reaction to me.

The real question is not *if* but *when* to tell your child about yourself. Here are a few "don'ts" for talking with your children:

Don't tell them stories you haven't first shared with your mate.

Don't use your children to dump out feelings that you have not resolved. (That means that if you are significantly angry, afraid, or guilty about something, you should seek healing before talking to your children.)

Don't use your feelings as an excuse to "cover up" events that shaped your child's life.

Don't use the talk as an excuse to gossip.

The second question about telling our children about our lives is not *if* but *how* to tell them. My objective in this book is to give other parents some ideas of how to talk with their children.

If you want your children to be open with you, it is a good idea to model openness. I value the openness that we have developed with the boys. This may not be everyone's ideal, but the options are to either be involved with them in the process or let them do it on their own. When I look at how many ways there are to run amuck, my choice is set. Additionally, this openness allows the children to learn their parents' views on sexuality.

Patience and being slow to speak can help us learn a great deal. One morning Rami jumped into the backseat of the station wagon ready to head to his third grade class. He was excited. "I learned a new song yesterday! Do you want to hear it?" He began to sing about French women's underpants. Jamie, who was in the front seat, turned quickly and began to shush him. With his more advanced age came the wisdom that some songs (and he obviously knew this one) were better kept from parental ears!

Meanwhile some childhood memory revived in my brain because this new discovery of Rami's was a rather old song. He knew others, and soon we had heard the glories of the burning of the school, "On Top of My Classroom," "Hi Ho, Hi Ho, It's Off to School We Go" (both versions), and other classics of the grade school underworld. Several poems were also forthcoming, as Rami continued to ignore his brother's vigorous nonverbal cues to cease and desist! Soon the conversation turned to which songs the teachers would permit and a good discussion of why those rules might be enforced. The topic was now open and discussions and additions occurred on many trips to or from school. By waiting to find out the whole picture, I had not only learned what was going on in third grade, but also how Rami evaluated it.

5. Why did you tell Jamie about your failures? Won't that discourage him or make him lose respect for you?

Failures are the basis of much learning. If a problem is too big for me to face, I want my children to be warned ahead of time. Perhaps they will do better than I did. I would like to be respected for learning from my mistakes. We don't need to create a false impression of ourselves to inspire respect in our children. The Bible's rigorous honesty in portraying the lives of the patriarchs should be our guide.

6. In the Leviticus 20 passage from your Bible study there are rules about menstruation. Why did you skip them and keep other rules governing sexual behavior?

It is accepted among Christians that not all the Old Testament applies to us today in the same way that it did in Moses' time. Still, after almost two thousand years of Christianity there is disagreement over which sections apply and which do not. There is agreement that the changes Jesus made are at the heart of the difference between the two covenants. Jesus did two things in regard to this Mosaic law that should help clarify why I picked one section to apply and the other to ignore.

First, Jesus teaches that in sexual conduct our thoughts count as do our actions. Both what we think and do is subject to the rules about adultery. In this way Christ strengthened the protective part of the law. Even our thoughts should protect each other's privacy and our sexuality. Therefore, when teaching Jamie, we read the protective part of the law. This establishes the minimal standard which the New Testament depends on in order to *expand* the protective function of men.

Second, Jesus' life reversed a very important state of affairs. Whereas in the Mosaic covenant the power of the curse was greater than the power of the blessing, precisely the opposite is true for Christ and his followers. According to the law of Moses, if anything pure or holy came in contact with something unholy, the holy side became unclean. Thus menstruation (blood) made the woman unclean. The unclean woman made the man who would have sex with her, or even touch her, unclean. People were to refrain from all unclean things, so the "keep away" rule was established.

Now when the woman who was unclean because of the issue of blood came to Jesus, things changed. This woman had a constant flow of blood for ten years. She probably had uterine fibroids, which meant that she was unclean and could not touch anyone without making them unclean. This is why she did not want Jesus to know she touched him. She appears to have figured out a way around the problem in order to keep Jesus from becoming unclean. Out of respect she decided to touch the hem of his garment since it got in the dust and so was probably unclean anyway. This might solve her dilemma of how to keep the curse (symbolized by uncleanness) from going to the Rabbi.

Jesus says that "the power went *out* of him" (emphasis mine). The curse did not come in to contaminate Christ but rather the blessing went out from Jesus to the woman. The blessing was now stronger than the curse. Amen! In so doing Jesus abolished the symbolic laws about uncleanness. They are no longer needed since the blessing became greater than the curse. Those who share in Jesus' blessing need not worry about becoming contaminated by unclean things. Jesus further proved this to be true by touching unclean lepers, dead bodies, feet, and even eating with sinners.

There is no contradiction in the way that Jesus affected the Mosaic law. In one case Christ increased the protection we were to provide, and in the second case he increased the protection provided to us by rendering the curse weaker than the blessing. That is why Christians are fond of singing, "Greater is he that is in us than he that is in the world." It is our good news. You may read the whole amazing story in Mark, chapter five.

7. What did you do differently with your second son, Rami?

One of the basic things to know about Rami is that he never walks anywhere. Rami runs, jumps, hops, or dances, but we don't expect him to walk. It is not that he does not think deeply about things, but rather that he thinks while in motion. So the first change to the story would be to add about two hundred questions of "What are we going to do now?" Consequently, when he chose to spend his three days in Sequoia National Park, we scheduled in many more activities with shorter talks between them.

Rami also becomes more silent when talking about feelings so it was necessary to ask more questions of him. I would ask, "What did you think of that?" or, "Does that seem strange?" or, "What does that make you think about?" When I asked, "Does it feel uncomfortable to talk about this?" I usually got a nod and not much else.

Because it is harder for Rami to talk about feelings, it was important to reassure him more often. That meant frequent pats on the back or hugs. The same thing would have interrupted Jamie's times of deep thought, but Rami thinks better while there is interaction with Dad.

The only content change with Rami was preparing a better organized Bible study. The one by the Penners, which I used with Jamie, was too much of an adult study. It was designed to correct common adult misconceptions on what the Bible says about sex. As a result, Jamie was confused by all the Old and New Testament roles and expectations for men and women. While that provided an interesting cultural and historical lesson, ancient Mideastern culture was not the subject for our trip. Rami's study focused more on principles for living and less on ancient history.

8. What connection does the father-and-son relationship have to homosexuality?

A hug is a symbol of belonging and closeness; then we let go. Fathers need to repeat that cycle with their children frequently. It helps children both to feel that they belong and to be independent. Fathers who treat their sons this way—both physically and emotionally—will go a long way towards helping their sons develop a healthy sexual attraction toward women.

Theories about the development of homosexuality in men are certainly controversial. As Earl Wilson points out, we have gone from a time when it was viewed as being caused by the mother, to thinking it is genetic, to some who now believe that it is just one of the various lifestyles one can choose. Interestingly the idea of choice is pushed most by those who, by adopting the genetic argument, insist they have no choice.

There has recently been an increasingly prevalent movement to attribute homosexual orientation to the *lack* of involvement by the boy's father during development. Gordon Dalbey goes farther by suggesting that it is not just the father but the community of men that are required for a boy to develop properly.

Dr. George Reekers points out that participation in team sports during puberty is a significant factor in the development of normal sexuality. I think that such team sports are one of the few ways in which men still train or interact with boys. In sports men pay close attention to what boys do, remember what they did before, keep records, encourage effort, and expect that the boys will make it. Regrettably, this experience must often *substitute* for their father's interest, which may be completely missing for the nonathletic boy. Even video games provide an alternative—however inadequate—to interacting with men. At least boys can fight against men on the screen.

At times this desire to be with men becomes so frustrated that it becomes sexualized as homosexuality.

9. Why do you mention sexual feelings between men?

Most of us are likely to have some homosexual feeling pop up along with many other feelings we wish we didn't have. Any of these feelings are difficult to mention to others and often lead to high levels of felt shame, guilt, and fear.

The purpose for talking about such feelings is to provide an alternative to the internal problem revealed by the presence of homoerotic feelings. This internal problem can usually be presumed to be a lack of close attachment to the object of the feelings. Therefore the best way to talk about homosexual feelings is to address the boy's need to bond with, be accepted by, and identify with the characteristics of the man towards whom the attraction exists.

Leanne Payne calls this attraction *cannibalism*. We want to consume or merge with the masculine in order to become masculine. But since we feel shame, we pick a shame-producing way of expressing our genuine need. Sex is the closest we can get to anyone in a physical way. However, sex does not bring closeness.

Unfortunately much child molesting comes about by the same misbegotten logic about sex equating closeness. Frequently, we find a father, grandfather, or, most often, stepfather trying to get close to the little boy or girl in his care. Not aware that he gets closer by protecting and nurturing, he gets close physically. So instead of closeness they end with shame. It makes me think of Adam and Eve's attempt to be close to (to be like) God and ending in shame. Shame leads to hiding, hiding to dissatisfaction, dissatisfaction to repetition, and repetition to shame. The force that leads to homosexual feelings, child molesting, or seeing how far you can get with a girl is exactly the same—shame. Its antidote is repentance, which leads to forgiveness and brings healing and acceptance.

Exploring homoerotic feelings always leads us to the shame of not being who we wish we were. Thus, being accepted by men and welcomed as one of them is the best prevention for this shame.

Changing one's sexual orientation is increasingly a concern for Christians only. Strangely enough, the Christian men who come to me for help in this area believe that the cure would result in them lusting like stallions after women instead of men. To me both are equally perversions of masculine sexuality. Both can be changed with great difficulty—but never by the person alone. I have given attention to the topic because there is hope for those dealing with homosexual feelings.

10. How does it feel to be telling the "whole world" about your private life?

Growing up as a missionary kid, I often had the feeling that the whole world was watching my life. Everywhere we went people remarked on what we did. "My! What well-behaved boys!" or, "Well! I didn't think a missionary's children would act like that!" In Bible school I wrote a paper called "Life in a Goldfish Bowl" and found out later that others have used the same expression for their experiences. The Christian community can be both kind and brutal. I have experienced and expect to experience more of both. One of the things I have learned as a missionary kid is that we teach by both example and precept. This book feels like a natural extension of those experiences.

11. You take a position that moderate drinking of alcohol is permitted by the Scriptures. Don't you see the problem of alcoholism?

One of my fears about writing an honest book is that the answer I gave to Jamie about drinking alcohol would be controversial and detract from the main message of the book. What I mean to point out is that fathers should talk to their sons, study the Scriptures with them, and explore their own family history with them. My answer to my son, that the Scriptures support drinking in moderation, could very well be wrong—but it is what I told Jamie at the time. Those who would like to understand this view could read *The Christian and Alcoholic Beverages: A Christian Perspective* by Kenneth Gentry.

A good case can be made against even moderate drinking. Amounts of alcohol as small as one drink per week have been linked to breast cancer, birth defects, traffic accidents, and the risk of developing alcoholism. With thirteen million alcoholics in the United States alone, this risk is no small problem. While there are many definitions of alcoholism, I prefer this one— you are an alcoholic if your drinking causes problems for you, your family, or your community.

I am appalled by the damage caused by alcoholism. In fact, being raised in an alcoholic family is the second most common cause for the damaged lives that come to me for counseling. The number one reason for damage to my clients is immoral sexual activity like incest and adultery. I don't see the Scriptures prohibiting either sex or drinking but rather placing very careful constraints on both. True, there are some people who should never drink and others who should never have sexual relations, but the focus of this book is on raising healthy children. Whether through abstinence or moderation, I can only hope more families take both of these issues seriously.

12. Why did you say so little to Jamie about pornography?

The simplest answer is that I didn't think about pornography very much at the time. Actually, it seems that pornography has become more of a social issue recently. Our church has run the interview between Dr. Dobson and serial killer Ted Bundy three times this year. This is more mention of pornography than I have heard in all my previous years in church.

Both boys have already been exposed to my views. Clearly, I have nothing good to say about pornography. I used to be somewhat indifferent to the magazines since I had little contact with them. Then I read the statistics of how many of these "models" had been sexually abused as children. That changed my perspective. I have a very low tolerance for exploiting victims.

I told my sons what I tell my friends if the subject comes up. "Say! I know some sexually abused women that have been molested by their fathers, neighbors, and ministers. One of them is doing so poorly emotionally that it is hard for her to keep going financially. Let's get some guys together, invite her over, and pay her to take her clothes off for us! What do you say?" My sons, like my friends, find such a suggestion very offensive, disgusting, and repulsive. So I say, "Well, if that is too messy for your tastes, let's pay some uncaring guys to do it for us. They can get rich finding the victims and bringing us the pictures." That usually settles the matter.

The clear duty of real men goes beyond "live and let live." We are mandated to protect widows, orphans, the alien, and all those who lack sustaining relationships. As long as men and boys fail to be protective, they will fall prey to the typical male sexual fantasy that sells these magazines and films. The fantasy, at its essence, amounts to someone simply losing control while trying to get enough of you. Most male sexual fantasies can be reduced to a variation on this theme.

These thoughts retain their appeal because they are partial solutions to a man's need to be masculine. Having the woman seek sexual gratification substitutes for the man's need to protect because there is no apparent victim. Since the woman is trying to get enough of the man sexually, pornography also substitutes sexual gratification for nurturing. Thus the man becomes the source of something good that gives him power. This creates an imaginary parallel to what a man could actually become.

Since in pornography the woman confers power on the man, the result is inherently frustrating. This dependency on women and the resulting frustration requires increased levels of violence and humiliation of the woman for each successive pornographic fantasy to work. The violence lets the man feel "powerful" again. This abuse of power leads ultimately to shame.

The only real solution is to teach boys that the source of their power is in the nurturing and protecting image of God created within them. When we express our essential nature, substitutes, like pornographic fantasies, lose their appeal.

13. What role do you see for the community of men in a boy's rite of passage?

For a rite of passage to be successful and complete, each boy needs to be welcomed into the community of men. This is best done by a group rather than a lone father as I did it. During his college days, Jamie pointed out to me this lack in his life and took steps to increase his involvement with other men. If, however, the boy sees his father as a representative of men, he will receive the acceptance by men through his father. This can be accomplished even without other men present. At any rate, involvement with men is a discipline the son must practice to join the community of men. Still, even in the absence of other men, each boy can come to know that he is a man with his father's help.

I was working alone to help Jamie through his rite of passage. I believe what I did would have been improved if I would have laid hands on Jamie on the cliffs above Cathedral Cove and said, "On behalf of the community of men, I, your father, bless you and welcome you as a man. May the Lord be with you always."

What an added blessing it would have been if upon our return all my friends would have shaken Jamie's hand and welcomed him among them as a man. Many other ideas can be added to these as each parent looks over the resources available to them and their child's personality. In these ways we can do the best we can with the children we have been given.

Questions and Answers about Talking with Your Child

———◆◆◆———

1. How do I help my child develop a normal sexual attitude?

All the men or women that I have met who are sexually obsessed have a common experience as children. Their opposite sex parent was either negative about their sexuality or ignored it totally, acting as though it did not exist. As a result, these adults have incessant fantasies characterized by being irresistible to the opposite sex. These obsessions make a poor substitute for validation of one's gender identity.

It has been said that the mind is the greatest erotic organ of the body. It is also the most teachable. This makes any idea of what would be normal sexual development of the mind almost impossible to determine. As a rule, the older we get, the more things become sexual to us. Words and actions begin to take on double meanings. At one extreme, one may be blind and naive, and at the other totally obsessed to the point that everything becomes sexual.

No attempt should be made to develop the erotic potential of a child's mind. Do not arouse desire before the means to fulfill it are at hand. There are plenty enough tensions to learn to live with, without that. You will find that I have tried systematically to avoid instructing my sons in ways to develop sexual arousal or pleasure. This will change as they approach mature sexual relations with their wives and such information becomes beneficial. In the meantime there will be enough input from their surroundings to keep them busy controlling their arousal.

Several persons with very sick minds (if not decidedly evil minds) have suggested that this sexual potential in children should be developed as early as possible. However, just because a girl has all the eggs that she will ever use present at birth does not mean that she is ready to be a mother from birth. We know that she is still not ready at ten or thirteen when pregnancy becomes biologically viable. Likewise, being able to throw a ball at eighteen months does not make one a major league pitcher. The capacity is there in a basic sense only. Much time and growth needs to take place before this ability is put to work. Meanwhile the job of parents and society is to protect these abilities and teach the child to protect them as well. It is very much like the reasons we would teach them not to jump off the roof while using their bed sheet as a parachute.

In the same way, even though children have the same nerve endings as adults, they do not possess adult sexuality, knowledge, or desires unless they have been severely abused sexually. Pedophiles constantly mistake children's ability to respond with desire or intention. They mistakenly conclude that the child "wanted it." This is a tragic mistake. Premature sexualization amounts to adding adult sexual components to a child ahead of when those aspects would develop normally. It is like teaching calculus in kindergarten; no good can come of it.

The other side of this matter is that children's sexuality is a very good thing when it develops on schedule. This means that as parents we have to work very hard to shield our children from the many factors that will sexualize them prematurely. At the same time we must guide, encourage, and support their sexuality at whatever time it emerges.

Children's sexuality can emerge at the strangest times. One such experience took place when our boys were in second and fourth grades. They were watching TV one night when a kissing scene came on the screen. They wiggled a lot, and then one of them turned to their mother and asked, "Why do our penises stand up when we watch people kissing on TV?"

Mom's inner reaction was shock that they would have put those two things together. But she tried to be calm when she gave her answer, while thinking that she would have to be more careful about what they watched in the future.

These are the crucial moments for children in sexual identity, not so much the planned education, as seeing how their parents respond to their bodies and sexuality. It is obvious that the planned times are essential, but how parents respond at unguarded or unplanned times carries much of the emotional message of how to feel about oneself.

What then is the message we should be prepared to give our children about themselves? Respect! Respect is the proper response. Respect for their feelings and ours as well. This may not be an easy balance to achieve. Children do not always know that they have hit on one of those subjects that make their parent's hair curl slightly at the roots. If the children sense that this is a difficult moment, then tensions can be even higher. Most children will avoid prolonging tension by creating a distraction.

The simplest way to show respect is to say something like, "That is an important question (subject, feeling, and so on) that makes me feel a little nervous to talk about because I'm not sure I know the right answer. Let me think a minute." Parents will relieve a lot of pressure on themselves if they get over the feeling that everything must be taken care of on the spot. If we do not have an answer, then we can say so and promise one later.

2. What should I do if my past has been more messed up than yours?

The central part of the rite of passage is introducing a boy to his place in history. Except for Scripture, nothing will help him more than an account of how your history has been redeemed. The worse your history has been the more room there will be for repentance and redemption. Redeeming your history requires that each aspect of your life be given to God for cleansing and use. God uses what we give him. God even used David's sin with Bathsheba to give us Solomon.

By the time your son grows up you should share an illustration of every major pitfall you want him to avoid. But let's be realistic. We fell into traps because we were fooled by something that seemed better than it was. That is the point. Our get-rich-quick, get-love-quick, get-popular-quick, or get-out-of-trouble-quick plan backfired on us. What we are regretting are the times we thought we could have fun, or even meet our needs, and then came up with troubles instead. We need to tell enough of the story so that our children can see how we were fooled by our expectations or those of others.

Then our children need to know how it felt to be tricked by our best plans. Did we get nothing? Did we get hurt? Did we get a mixed outcome of good and bad? (Even some heinous things can turn out that way.)

Finally, we need to describe the alternatives we have found since our painful lessons. What can you do or recommend to help your son inherit the good and avoid the bad outcomes? How can you deal with incredible loneliness without drugs, for instance?

As you are talking about these things, be sensitive to how fast your children are learning what you are telling. Attentive faces, questions, and moving closer to you signal that the child is handling your talk well. Incessant squirming, withdrawing, anger, or moving away indicate that you are saying too much for now. Children will usually tell a receptive parent when something is too much or not enough. Pay attention to the messages that they give when you speak with them.

There are some approaches that will not help. Most of them focus on regrets or guilt to the exclusion of a positive alternative. A few men give the impression that they are sorry what they did was "bad," because if they could, they would do it again. This usually comes out in some nostalgia about wild days. This is double-minded talk. Such a man should not think that he can teach his son anything. No matter what he says, the double-minded message comes through. The message, "it is your obligation to be good and miss out on life," does not convince anyone.

Such men usually accuse their children or wives of being or plotting to do all manner of things the man sees as evil but secretly wants to do himself. Their wives visit churches and Christian bookstores trying to figure out how to get their husbands to read books like this one. But the double-minded man is unstable and "is a splintered cane that will run into a man's hand and pierce it if he leans on it" (an ancient Assyrian taunt).

Those who are serious about teaching their sons will find that almost all of the "bad things" in their past will fall into one of three categories: bad judgment, trauma, or addiction. Let us consider them separately for a moment. Bad judgments are the times that we have deliberately done the wrong thing. Traumas are bad things that happened to us that hurt us and made us feel powerless. Addictions are experiences we repeat, regardless of their cost, to change the way we feel. The outcome of addictions is that we eventually feel powerless to stop. There are addictions to chemicals, sex, activities, and people (relationships).

As you have seen in this book, it is my belief that children should be prepared to deal with bad judgment, trauma, and addiction. If you are not coping well with one of these, *please get help*. Let your child know that you are getting help. If you are coping well, then teach your answers to your son. What works for you might not work for him, but he will at least know that there are solutions to the problems he may one day face.

For example, let us say that a man has struggled for years with pornography. As a child, he may have been traumatized by exposure to his uncle's pornography. Now he has a sexual addiction that causes him to rent videos that cause him shame. Additionally, he has left pornography around the house where his children have found it, which shows a lack of judgment.

There are several ways to handle the situation. Denying the problem is the worst, as that prevents anyone in his family from protecting themselves from the consequences. The next best alternative is to admit the problem even if he can't or won't do anything about it. At least others have permission to escape (though they rarely would without his help). The next level for growth is actively finding help. He and his family will be busy for a while. The final level of victory is sharing with his child the lessons and healing he reached. That is the main focus of this book. With these lessons comes the power to become a protective and nurturing man.

3. How do I tell my son that he was conceived before marriage?

Once again we return to the redemption of our personal histories. When sinful aspects of our behavior have been confessed and forgiven, God is free to bring glory to himself out of what was once shameful. Once again we must examine ourselves for the answer.

As a psychologist, I can answer a question with a question. What do you *really* believe about your son's conception before marriage? This is a place where every man needs a good friend to talk things over. Tell the whole story to your friend. Give your reasons why things turned out as they did. List the good and bad points of the story. Have your friend point out if you are using double-talk, or trying to fool yourself. This should help you be honest and practice talking about your life.

When your son is seven or eight years old, you may create an opportunity to talk with him about his conception. Perhaps some day when you are working on his pitch for Little League, you can point out that there are good and bad parts to his throw. Maybe he has a good kick, but his release is too high. Then afterwards while you are having a soft drink, you could say, "Your pitching is coming along nicely, but it still has some bad parts along with the good parts."

He might squirm a bit and say, "I try to do the release right."

You might smile and say, "That's right, but it still ends up in Mr. Mooney's yard sometimes." After a bit more conversation, you might add: "Well, there are good and bad parts to things I do too. Like yesterday I went to the grocery store to buy this soft drink, and I wrote down the right amount of money on the check, but I put the name of the wrong grocery store. I sure was embarrassed!

"Sometimes," you might say, "the good and the bad parts of what I do have much bigger results than just having to rewrite a check. Probably the biggest time like that was the time you were conceived. Do you remember what *conceived* means?"

And so you are off to tell him about the really good part of having him for a son along with whatever problems he can understand at his age. He would understand things like who was upset at first and how things changed. Finally you could point out to him how he could retain the good portions of your experience for himself and avoid the negative sides as he grows up.

These conversations are not one-time events. Expect that you will need to repeat them with every level of development your child achieves. If your home is healthy, your son should be able to point out to you how lessons he is learning at school, church, or from a friend's experiences apply to you, and this lesson you are teaching him.

During grade school, the focus of talks between father and son will be on feeling secure and wanted. During junior high, it will be more on following rules. During high school, issues of your inner conflicts and how you decided what was important will be the focus of your talks. Spreading these talks over ten years will make it easier for both of you. The hardest part is the first plunge, so talk that over with a friend and your wife to get the jitters out of your system.

4. When is therapy called for?

Therapy (short for psychotherapy) means "the treatment of the soul." To answer the question, it might help to point out the difference between three similar procedures: therapy, healing, and counseling.

Counseling is providing solutions for known problems to people who are able to implement these solutions. Counseling is giving good, helpful advice. Counseling is the exercising of wisdom.

Healing is the removing of pain or damage left by some injury. Our souls, bodies, and spirits can, and often are, injured. Most mental illnesses represent an attempt to avoid such pain. Healing will not remove the scar, only the pain and destructiveness of the wound. Every time our souls are injured, they need healing. Sometimes we need good counsel to show us how, and other times we already know what to do from our previous experience.

Psychotherapy is a method of figuring out what damage has been done to the soul. It is useful when we don't know what hurts us, and so we cannot even get good counsel. Another sign that therapy is needed is when apparently good counsel does no good when we try to apply it to our lives. Therapy should be considered whenever attempts to correct problems repeatedly end in helplessness, frustration, confusion, or passivity.

The best guideline for seeking help, whether counseling, healing, or therapy, is your own feeling that you could use some help just now. Sure, there are people who push individuality as far as it will go. Some people will pull their own teeth or take two aspirins when they have a heart attack, but God meant us to give and receive help from each other. Don't wait until you absolutely need help to seek some.

5. Could you provide a simple list of how-to steps for other fathers to follow when talking to their sons?

Actually, I don't want to. I would rather you be inspired to try and make your own discoveries and mistakes. Nevertheless, here is a short list.

1. Repeat lessons often.
2. Try out your approach on a friend and on your wife before you talk to your child.
3. Fast and pray ahead of time.
4. Write down the major points of family history.
   A. Events that shaped the child's life
   B. People who shaped the child's life
   C. Strengths and weaknesses of the family
   D. Victories your family has achieved
   E. Victories still waiting to be achieved
5. Go someplace comfortable to talk.
6. Listen to your children.
7. Repeat lessons often.

You are preparing your children for life. Leading your son through a rite of passage means placing in him an understanding of his part in history. He must understand that from now on he bears ever-increasing responsibility for how his life shapes history. It has been said repeatedly that each generation has faced more choices than the last. There are, at least, innumerable choices to be made these days. We need to help our children be good at making choices.

There is more involved here than simply making children choose between the alternatives that we provide. They often need to expand their thinking beyond choices set in front of them. Very often there are not good options in the list provided to them or to us. Particularly if we want to be Christians in our society, we need to create some of our own options; however, everyone—Christian and non-Christian—needs this ability.

Rigid parents need to hear this more than others. The problem I have is that I want my children to do the right thing, and often they do not. The fastest way to correct them is to tell them what is right, and make sure that they do exactly as they are told with no arguing. That is the rigid solution. It works best with grade-school-aged children. Younger children do not understand instructions, and older children tend to rebel. So, no sooner are parents starting to feel that they are getting results than it all blows up in their face.

When our society tells us that a girl's value is decided by how pretty she is, or that a boy's value rests on how well he performs, we need to think of different options than those provided to us. What do we do when a large section of our society believes that the way for children to become adults is to get rid of their virginity (if they are fortunate enough to still have it by their teens)? If their virginity is already gone, then the next step is getting pregnant. Don't we want our children to find other options than those that are provided to them?

These options we create do not come out of the air. They come from our deepest guiding principles for life, whether those values are good or bad. They show the kind of people we are. If at a deep level we are personally connected with God, then with each temptation there is a way of escape. This is not just a matter of inspiration or mystical guidance—although that helps. There is also a need to have guidelines. We need to be familiar with Scripture, our guide to decision making, in order to make wise options available.

Finding these options will take the best of our creativity, *plus* our children's. No matter how involved we are with them now, they will still have to live and solve problems when we are not around. This leaves us no alternative but to teach them to think of their own options. Sometimes we may not be there when they need us, or we may be too far behind in preparing them for the problems that they are facing. We tend to expect our children to solve problems at the same age that we did, or somehow miss them altogether.

6. How do you apply your policy of giving your children options in real situations?

An example of these principles in action began with a family vacation in the woods and lakes of northern Minnesota. The boys' uncle taught them the fine art of knocking over tin cans with a .22, and they both decided that they wanted a gun. They were not about to be talked out of their desire by a practical consideration like the difficulty of finding a place to shoot a gun in a big metropolitan area like Los Angeles. To buy some time I told them that they could choose to have a gun or some other things when they each turned thirteen. For me this meant coming up with something more appealing than a gun by that time.

A little careful listening to a five- and seven-year-old talk about guns revealed that *power* was the big attraction. Not simple brute power, but power to move and control from a distance. A boy with a gun can make a can move from an impressive distance. This suggested to me that a remote control plane would be a good second choice for a thirteen-year-old. This idea was greeted with great enthusiasm while the virtues of each choice were vigorously debated. Later they suggested the additional choice of a remote control programmable robot. This strengthened my idea that controlling things was a major part of the gun's appeal. The robot was disqualified by its price tag— maybe when they have kids it will be different.

Now, some of you might still be wondering why I don't just exert my parental authority and say no. Why not simply say that there will be no gun? Well, there are very few times when I will resort to a straight parental no. What do my children gain out of that except to know that their dad is strong-willed? There are three reasons to avoid this approach when possible.

First is the practical point that my saying no does not help my sons develop their judgment. In less than two decades from their first appearance on earth they will be making these decisions for themselves. Training them to make wise choices needs to start very young.

Second, the more arbitrary rules I set down, the more they will have to rebel about later. Since having rebellious teens does not appeal to me, I avoid appearing arbitrary whenever possible.

The third reason to avoid being arbitrary in saying no emerges in large part from my theology. Further, this belief is what creates the challenge to come up with a better alternative than the one to which I would say no. You see, I believe that God did not make rules and say no to things out of the sheer joy of throwing power around or keeping us from having fun. That approach implies that sin is the best way to live and those of us saps who follow God just miss the good life. On the contrary, I believe that for every time that God says no he has an alternate and much improved way to meet our needs. To apply this way of thinking to myself means that I face the challenge of finding, or helping the boys find, a better way to handle each situation in which I might say no.

7. How do parents prepare to confront the power of a high school student who can physically overpower them?

The person who empowers is greater than the one who limits power. Most of us have met clerks in government offices who took advantage of their power by restricting our actions. That is very frustrating. Most of us, by contrast, remember the first time we were given the car keys as an exhilarating moment.

If you endeavor to be a godly father, your children should recognize you as a source of service and power by the time they have power of their own. Adolescence then becomes a time of teaching children how to use their power to serve and protect others.

The devil runs a top-down power scheme that is controlled by and serves the one at the top. He is the foundation and support of *all* top-down power schemes.

In God's authority structure the higher up you go the more people you must serve. We are cautioned against climbing too high as the demands of service require that we are judged more severely.

Providing approval, resources, and permission to make decisions and mistakes is the main way we give power to teens. If you rely on threats and intimidation to control your children, you are indeed in trouble when they decide to rebel. By using threats you have taught them to trust the dark side for strength, and they will probably pay you back in kind.

There are children who, all on their own, choose to be fools. This is a risk all parents take. Treat a fool as his folly deserves. By all means do not save them from the consequences of their own actions. That is one of the few ways they might learn to seek wisdom.

8. How should age and developmental stages affect the levels of parental affection with children?

Some developmental stages are easy to see and follow. When children become too heavy, it is time to stop showing affection by carrying them or sitting them on your lap. Bath times, which also involve some affectionate play, stop as children are able to bathe and dress themselves. From that time on affection with nudity should be avoided.

It is a good guideline to keep the same level of affection regardless of whether you are alone with the child or others such as siblings or your spouse are present.

Another guideline is to use the same sort of kissing and hugging for both sons and daughters. If you kiss your daughter, kiss your son the same way and do the same with hugs. It helps to keep straight what is affection and what is sexual. I am writing for people who can keep sex out of relationships with their children, but if you cannot keep that straight, get some help.

Children's need for affection does not decrease very much from birth through adolescence. Children pick up their parents' reluctance to approach them and withdraw from kisses if they sense that there is something suspect about what is going on. Social and peer pressure can also have the same result. This is the same peer pressure that encourages them to do other unhealthy things and should be treated accordingly. Build your child's self-esteem enough that he can tell his friends, "I'm sorry affection makes you uncomfortable."

9. Does hugging sons at home help them control themselves with girls?

This is an area where both parents can have an influence. Children who feel they are attractive and acceptable to their mother and father will be much more secure with the opposite sex. This helps to reduce craving for contact *from* others and replace it with a natural flow of acceptance and approval *towards* others. There is nothing we can give our children that will make them more attractive to their peers during adolescence than the quiet assurance that they can give and receive affection.

One of the few strong objections I have to Connie Marshner's book *Decent Exposure* is her statement, "Boys will be boys (unless girls decide to be girls.)"[1] Although I agree with her attempt to teach girls to protect themselves, this statement promotes a totally perverted view of boys. What she is inadvertently saying is "Boys are lechers by nature while girls are not."

A biblical view of men shows them to be (1) protectors and (2) nurturers. The expression "Boys will be boys" implies that their destiny is to be aggressors and users. This teaching is precisely the opposite of the scriptural mandate. Boys need to be taught the truth about themselves, namely that their destiny is to be protectors and caretakers in the kingdom of the Most High God.

Now, let's return to the question of meeting your son's needs for affection as a way of keeping him from feeling so deprived that he might doubt whether a girl or boy would want to be close to him. Sons who are appropriately and regularly hugged, kissed, and touched are, in my opinion, more able to see themselves as the source of something good than in terrible need to receive care from a girl.

Part of the appeal of fathering a child, for instance, is the feeling of being the source of something good, something important that others care about a great deal. Unfortunately, the "boy turned man" that has not learned to protect and nurture will continue to seek acceptance through sex and leave his children for someone else to serve and protect. In fact, most boys don't think about serving and protecting at all, unless they are learning the motto for the police department or armed forces. We need to bring the motto home again.

10. What is the difference between masculinity and femininity?

When masculinity is defined as protecting and nurturing, as in this book, it is understandable that many people ask how that differs from femininity. I would answer that femininity is nurturing and protecting, but not necessarily in that order. Rather, there is a tendency for women to clump the two together and protect and nurture at the same time. Men separate the two into different categories and different activities.

Christians believe that Christ exemplified complete humanity. Thus when the spirit of Christ (protection/keeping and nurture/service) is expressed through a man, it becomes the soul satisfying essence of masculinity. The same spirit expressing the same virtues through a woman becomes the quintessence of femininity.

Imagine the same sweet and rich melody being played on a flute and a cello. The tune is identical but the sound is magnificently different. So it is when the men and women protect and nurture, there is no confusing the two different instruments as they play.

11. What do I tell my children if I used drugs?

Tell them how close you are to using drugs again, then answer all their questions. Remember to let God redeem and use every aspect of your history. There is no point in letting it go to waste.

12. What do you have to say about fathers and daughters?

Next to being asked why we need another book on sex, this is the question I hear most often. I have had many unique experiences which give me some perspective on daughters. As an elder I have adopted several daughters and shared the joy of raising them. (See my other book *Life Passages for Men* for an understanding of elders and the kind of role they play.) In addition, my counseling work affords me a Monday morning quarterback look at the work of other fathers with their daughters. All these experiences, plus nieces, neighbors, and little friends, have given me clues to what is important for girls.

Fathers with deceased or delinquent wives want to know what they should do about their daughter's rite of passage. Girls need the same preparation boys do, and except for welcoming her into the community of women, a father is free to teach her about her history and people—including her mother. Whatever the mother's influence, the girl needs to know that everything is open to being redeemed if we will tell the truth about it. A girl's femininity needs her father's appreciation, protection, and respect, but that is not all a girl needs.

Dawna Marie (who calls me "Yogurt Cow" because of a silly game we made up) has shown me that she wants her ideas understood. Barbara does not like to be ignored. Jodi lets me know how important it is to be held or have her back scratched —even if she is six. Mimi appreciates it when I'm fair with her (others are welcome to be fair with her as well). Sophia would prefer not to be teased. Emily wants all her questions answered. She asks, "Why are you bald?" "Why are you so old when mommies never get old?" Mary wants to know that she can be feminine without having to pretend to be afraid of every bug. Samara wants to know that boys won't get away with breaking the rules just because they are more aggressive than she is. Sandy needs to know that just because her parents let her do something doesn't mean it is allowed in our house. As they pass through their thirteenth year, all girls want someone to notice the things that make them cute, especially if the boys aren't paying attention to them.

Several adult women have honored me by adopting me as a father. They seem glad to see a masculinity in action which is protecting and nurturing. It makes their souls prosper. I'll say this though—as many step-fathers can tell you—when a father doesn't start with the poopy diapers and the spit-up running down his neck (while he is wondering where he put that clean diaper), it is harder to keep protecting and nurturing in focus all the time.

This book has been about talking, listening, hugging, and turning a father's heart towards his children. It has been about forming a child's identity and taking him or her through a rite of passage into a new identity even larger than before. It is about making a mark on history. If it works for you and your son or daughter, be sure to tell someone.

NOTES

FOUR
The Owner's Manual

1. H. Norman Wright and Clifford and Joyce Penner, *In Touch with Each Other* (Omaha, NE: Family Concern, 1976), 43-45.

SIX
Yield?

1. Russell Baker, *Growing Up* (New York: Congdon and Weed, 1982).

SEVEN
Collisions

1. Dean Kliewer, "Managing Sexual Feelings in the Christian Community," *Journal of Psychology and Christianity* 5.4 (1986):50-65.

THIRTEEN
*Questions and Answers
about Talking with Your Child*

1. Connie Marshner, *Decent Exposure: How to Teach Your Children about Sex* (Brentwood, TN: Wolgemuth & Hyatt, 1988).

APPENDIX

A

RESOURCES

ADULT SEXUALITY
Penner, Clifford and Joyce Penner. *The Gift of Sex.* Waco, TX: Word, 1981.
Wright, H. Norman, Clifford Penner and Joyce Penner. *In Touch with Each Other.* Omaha, NE: Family Concern, 1976.

ALCOHOL AND DRUGS
Baucom, John Q. *Help Your Children Say No to Drugs.* Grand Rapids, MI: Pyranee, 1987.
Bustanoby, Andrae S. *The Wrath of Grapes: Drinking and the Church Divided.* Grand Rapids, MI: Baker, 1987.
Gentry, Kenneth L. *The Christian and Alcoholic Beverages: A Biblical Perspective.* Grand Rapids, MI: Baker, 1986.
Seixas, Judith S. and Geraldine Youcha. *Children of Alcoholics: A Survival Manual.* New York: Harper & Row, 1985.
Strack, Jay. *Drugs and Drinking.* Nashville, TN Thomas Nelson, 1985.

CHILD SEXUALITY
Penner, Clifford and Joyce Penner. *A Gift for All Ages.* Waco, TX: Word, 1986.

CHRISTIAN SEXUALITY
Dillow, Joseph C. *Solomon on Sex.* Nashville, TN: Thomas Nelson, 1977.
Smedes, Lewis B. *Sex for Christians.* Grand Rapids, MI: Eerdmans, 1976.
Trobisch, Walter. *I Loved a Girl.* New York: Harper Chapel, 1963.

Trobisch, Walter. *I Married You*. New York: Harper & Row, 1971.

Vertefeuille, John. *Sexual Chaos: The Personal and Social Consequences of the Sexual Revolution*. Westchester, IL: Crossway, 1988.

FEELINGS

Gordon, Thomas, Ph.D. *Parent Effectiveness Training*. New York: Plume, 1970.

McDowell, Josh. *Love Dad*. Dallas, TX: Word, 1988.

Trobisch, Walter. *Living with Unfulfilled Desires*. Downers Grove, IL: InterVarsity Press, 1979.

Trobisch, Walter. *Love IS a Feeling to Be Learned*. Downers Grove, IL: InterVarsity Press, 1971.

HOME LIFE

Canfield, Ken R. *The 7 Secrets of Effective Fathers*. Wheaton, IL: Tyndale House Publishers, 1992.

McDowell, Josh and Dr. Norm Wakefield. *The Dad Difference*. San Bernadino, CA: Here's Life Publishers, 1989.

Wangerin, Walter, Jr. *As for Me and My House*. Nashville, TN: Thomas Nelson, 1987.

MASCULINITY

Dalbey, Gordon. *Healing the Masculine Soul*. Waco, TX: Word Books, 1988.

Payne, Leanne. *Crisis in Masculinity*. Westchester, IL: Crossway Books, 1985.

Trobisch, Walter and Gordon MacDonald. *All a Man Can Be & What a Woman Should Know*. Downers Grove, IL: InterVarsity Press, 1983.

Weber, Stu. *Tender Warrior*. Portland, OR: Multnomah Books, 1993.

Wilder, E. James. *Life Passages for Men*. Ann Arbor, MI: Servant, 1993.

MASTURBATION

Trobisch, Walter and Ingrid Trobisch. *My Beautiful Feeling*. Downers Grove, IL: InterVarsity Press, 1976.

PUBERTY & ADOLESCENCE

Arp, Claudia. *Almost 13: Shaping Your Child's Teenage Years Today*. Nashville, TN: Thomas Nelson, 1986.

Dobson, James. *Preparing for Adolescence*. Ventura, CA: Regal Books, 1978.

Peterson, Eugene H. *Growing Up with Your Teenager*. Old Tappan, NJ: Revell, 1988.

SEXUAL PROBLEMS

Bahnsen, Greg L. *Homosexuality: A Biblical View.* Phillipsburg, NJ: Presbyterian & Reformed Publishing, 1978.

Belliveau, Fred and Lin Richter. *Understanding Human Sexual Inadequacy.* New York: Bantam, 1970.

Comiskey, Andrew. *Pursuing Sexual Wholeness.* Wheaton, IL: Creation House, 1989.

Gil, Eliana Ph.D. *Outgrowing the Pain: A Book for and about Adults Abused as Children.* New York: Dell, 1983.

Wilson, Earl D. *A Silence to Be Broken.* Portland, OR: Multnomah, 1986.

Wilson, Earl D. *Sexual Sanity.* Downers Grove, IL: InterVarsity Press, 1984.

TELLING YOUR CHILDREN ABOUT SEX

Ketterman, Grace M. *How to Teach Your Children about Sex.* Old Tappan, NJ: Power, 1981.

Marshner, Connie. *Decent Exposure: How to Teach Your Children about Sex.* Brentwood, TN: Wolgemuth & Hyatt, 1988.

Mayo, Mary Ann. *Parent's Guide to Sex Education.* Grand Rapids, MI: Pyranee, 1986.

McDowell, Josh and Dick Day. *Why Wait? What You Need to Know about the Teen Sexual Crisis.* San Bernardino, CA: Here's Life, 1987.

TOPICS FOR THE TRIP

Jamie's List
1. Who should you like (things about a girl)
2. What puberty means (things about it)
3. Drugs, alcohol, and smoking
4. Who should you hang out with
5. School
6. How old do you have to be to date
7. Your enemies
8. Rock and roll
9. Dressing—clothes
10. Life's ambition

Dad's List
Puberty
basic biology
erections
nocturnal emissions
menstruation
self-stimulation

emotional instability
acne

Adolescence
independence
self-control
responsibility
my experience
Kitty's experience
peers
junior high—raw power—challenge your peers
senior high—attraction and control—challenge adults
conflict with parents
Kitty's problems letting go
my problem with withdrawal and passivity

Sex
basic biology
birth control
abortion
conception
fertility
venereal disease
learning your sexual response
relaxation/anxiety/quickies
petting
sexual exposure/myths/media
pleasure
homosexuality
bestiality
rape
what the Bible has to say on sex
names for genitals—vulgar/slang/pet names

Dating and Sexuality
relating to women as friends

sex versus communication

sex and affection

affection without sex

petting, excitement, and sex, instead of getting to know each other

attraction and sex are easy and normal—relationships are harder

respect for others—how Jesus would see them

dating

group dating

solo dating

dating to have fun versus dating to find a wife

dealing with damaged people

premature sexualization

abuse and rape

inability to distinguish sex from affection

fear of rejection

dependency

making mistakes—self-consciousness versus confidence

grandparents' dating experience

sensitivity and listening

strength and assertiveness

falling in love

Anecdotes

stories and trivia to make things more relaxed and memorable

BIBLE STUDY GUIDE

1. Sexuality is part of God's creation. (Gn 1:26-28; 5:1-2; 2:24-25)

2. The husband-wife sexual relationship symbolizes God's relationships with humankind. (Eph 5:21-32; Rv 19:6-7)

3. The biblical writers assume married couples enjoy sexual pleasure. (Sg 1:1-4; Eccl 9:7-10; 1 Cor 7:3-5)

4. Barriers between the sexes are broken down. (Gal 3:28)

5. There are rules surrounding sex. (Lv 20:1-21; Sg 2:7)
   A. Parents should protect their children from sexual activity. (Lv 19:29; 20:1-3)
   B. Society and each person in it have an obligation to protect children. (Lv 20:4-5)
   C. Caring for family means no sex with relatives by blood or marriage. (Lv 20:11-21)
   D. Human sexuality is to be with other human beings only —not animals. (Lv 20:15-16)
   E. No homosexuality is allowed. (Lv 20:13-14)

   F. We should avoid exposing nudity. (Lv 20:17)
   G. Sex is reserved for marriage partners. (Lv 20:10)
   H. Do not arouse sexual desire where it does not belong. (Sg 2:7)

6. Following God is important. (Dt 27:15-28:68)

Another Book of Interest by the Author

Life Passages for Men
Understanding the Stages of a Man's Life
E. James Wilder

We assume men grow up. But do they? Dr. Jim Wilder contends that many men never fully mature because they fail to negotiate the passage from boyhood to manhood. An almost equally tragic trend occurs when men never make the transition to grandfathers and elders in their families, churches, and wider communities.

One way to reverse these trends, says Dr. Wilder, is by helping men and women alike understand the stages in a man's life, along with his unique place in history, and then showing men creative ways to negotiate the passage from one stage to the next. With this wisdom, a man can reach maturity as a father who is a life-giver and later as an elder who blesses the church and fathers spiritual children. He can become a man of destiny. **$8.99**